MICROWAVE COOKING

Edited by
Cecilia Norman

CONTENTS

This edition first published 1978 by
Octopus Books Limited
59 Grosvenor Street, London W1

© 1978 Octopus Books Limited

Reprinted 1983

ISBN 0 7064 0665 6

Produced and printed in Hong Kong by
Mandarin Publishers Limited
22a Westlands Road, Quarry Bay

Frontispiece: QUICHE LORRAINE (*page 30*)

Weights and Measures

All measurements in this book are based on Imperial weights and measures, with American equivalents given in parenthesis.

Measurements in *weight* in the Imperial and American system are the same. Measurements in *volume* are different, and the following table shows the equivalents:

Spoon measurements

Imperial	U.S.
1 tablespoon	1 tablespoon
1½ tablespoons	2 tablespoons
2 tablespoons	3 tablespoons (abbrev: T)

Level spoon measurements are used in all the recipes.

Liquid measurements

1 Imperial pint	20 fluid ounces
1 American pint	16 fluid ounces
1 American cup	8 fluid ounces

INTRODUCTION

Microwave cookery is becoming extremely popular because of its speed and cleanliness, and also because of its immense saving in fuel costs. Obviously you must have the use of a microwave oven before you can cook by this method. The choice of models now available is very wide, but they all cook in the same way and are similar in appearance.

When a microwave oven is switched on, the magnetron which is the heart of the oven, generates waves which pass through a channel into the cavity, oscillating at great speed. These waves pass through the food causing the molecules to agitate, thus producing heat. If you rub your hands together, you can feel the warmth created by friction and microwave cookery works in the same way.

When the machine stops or is switched off, these microwaves stop and no longer remain in the food. The best comparison is to consider an electric light bulb. When the current is switched off, no light rays remain in the room.

All microwave ovens are fitted with a number of safety devices. These ensure that the machine switches off as soon as the door is opened. The instruction leaflet supplied with every new oven will give full details, but if you are buying a secondhand oven, it is advisable to have it tested by a service agent just in case the door has been slightly damaged or become misaligned.

Microwave ovens are controlled solely by time switches. As there are no heated elements, the oven doesn't become hot. The latest models have variable control switches which enable the electrical output to be adjusted to provide the equivalent of conventional settings. There are two methods by which manufacturers arrange this. Either the usual high speed is interrupted by short imperceptible rest periods, or the wave lengths are altered to provide continuous but lower speed friction cooking.

When buying a microwave oven it is a matter of getting what you pay for and adapting your cooking habits accordingly. Some homes rely heavily on a cooker fitted with an automatic timer, while others have no use for this at all. So it is with the microwave oven. If you buy a luxury model, you will be able to control the cooking at the touch of an electronic button. If you buy a cheaper model you will obtain just as good results by switching on and off manually, and turning the dishes from time to time. However, if you have a model with the revolving turntable, ignore instructions for 'turning' given in the recipes.

It is impossible to describe all the different ovens on the market and it would be wise for you to consider your personal cookery requirements. Do you need a built-in grill or an oven that keeps food warm? What sort of cooking do you do? Mainly thawing and reheating frozen foods or generally preparing fresh foods? Do you frequently prepare casseroles and egg custards or are your meals mainly quickly prepared dishes? Each manufacturer produces a range of these appliances, so that you can select your favourite according to your needs.

The food in a microwave oven does not cook by radiant heat so that no browning takes place. Some ovens have a built-in grill which operates concurrently or separately to provide this missing finishing touch to your dishes. Otherwise the conventional grill will do the job. A browning skillet is now an obtainable accessory with most ovens, and this combined with even the cheapest model can cope with nearly every cooking requirement. There is no direct heat in a microwave oven so fat cannot burn on. All that is required to keep the oven clean is a wipe over with a damp cloth, moistened with washing up liquid and a soft cloth to dry and shine the lining. Some base plates are removable for more thorough cleaning and if these are made of glass, they can be scoured in the normal way. Washing, cooking and serving dishes will require little effort to clean, because food is unlikely to stick. Paper or paper plates which are also suitable in microwave ovens, can be thrown away after use.

TOLHOUSE BAKED BEANS (page 63)

The dishes, plates and bowls that are already in your cupboard will most likely be suitable and the best choice will be those least likely to absorb any microwave energy themselves. Remember that you will be able to cook in your serving dishes so that saucepans become superfluous. You could not use saucepans in any case since they are generally made of metal and this is almost forbidden in the microwave oven.

All the recipes refer to heat resistant dishes, bowls or casseroles. This does not include the heavy cast iron or enamelled pans often used in the conventional oven. Suitable materials include china, glass, ceramics, cardboard, paper, some plastics, wood and straw. Most china and ceramics are safe to use and you only need to carry out this simple test once to be sure. Put a half filled glass of water in the dish. Cook for 1 minute. The water should then be much hotter than the edge of the dish. If the dish is hotter than the water, it will not be microwave proof for any length of time. In practice, I have never had a breakage over the many years I have been microwave cooking. In addition to ovenproof glass, you can use any type that is resistant to high temperature liquids. Drinks and nightcaps can be heated in goblets without risk. Pyroflam slows down the microwave cooking process, but food cooked in the microwave oven in items from this range can then be kept hot on the conventional hob or placed directly under the grill.

Browning skillets are produced in different shapes and sizes. When pre-heated empty in the microwave oven for a few minutes, the skillet reaches a temperature of 600°F 315°C, enabling chops and steaks to be seared and browned. The skillet can also be used without pre-heating for general microwave cookery and has the added advantage of being usable in the conventional oven. Where recipes in this book indicate the use of the browning skillet the pre-heating time refers to the 9½ inch size. Smaller sizes will only require 2½ minutes pre-heating.

Plastics are made from a variety of polymers. In general, plastic dishes that are dishwasher proof may be used for warming food in the microwave oven, but when ingredients such as butter or sugar predominate, the high temperature reached would damage the plastic. Boilable bowls made from polypropylene and mainly used for puddings and sauces, have a fairly long microwave life. Tupperware should only be used for warming or for the initial stages of thawing. Don't use yogurt pots or polystyrene dishes, but do make use of plastic cling film whenever you want to hasten cooking foods which need to be kept moist. It seals in the heat and the trapped steam speeds up cooking. Remember plastic film will burst if stretched too tightly, so cover the dish loosely and you will be pleased with the results. Food covered this way will be perfectly sealed against germs. Boilable bags can be used safely provided they are punctured to allow the steam to escape otherwise they may explode. Polythene freezer bags can be used for preliminary defrosting when taken straight from the freezer but remember to remove the metal closure tag.

It is most important to remember that metal can almost never be used in a microwave oven. Metal trim of any kind is likely to cause 'arcing' and may damage the magnetron. Rims of metal trimmed cups and saucers would be permanently discoloured and metal of any kind which touched the internal surface of the oven would cause 'pitting'. Above all, food placed in a metal dish would not heat, because the metal would screen out the microwaves.

Unless stated by the manufacturers, the *only* time when metal may be used is where the mass of food is far greater than the quantity of metal. Skewers in poultry are permissible provided they do not touch the oven walls. Small pieces of aluminium foil twisted round the wing tips or legs of poultry can prevent overcooking and if you find one section of food is cooking faster than it should, it can be covered with a small piece of foil.

At the beginning of each chapter you will find cookery tips to help you to get the best out of your microwave cooker. Of course you will have to experiment to find out how it can make your life so much easier, but once used to it, you will never want to part with this appliance. It takes several months to learn how to cook conventionally, so please give yourself a week or two to learn to cook by microwave.

Oven settings and cooking times

Timings of microwave cookery cannot be precise, since much depends on the density and composition of the food and on its starting temperature. For example, some ingredients may have come straight from the freezer or the refrigerator and will take longer to cook. Regard also has to be given to the quantity of food being cooked at any one time and voltage fluctuations.

Just as conventional cookers vary in temperature at particular settings, so microwave ovens vary in speed of cooking. Try out a recipe first, compare the time it takes with that given in the recipe, then adjust cooking times according to your oven's performance throughout the book. The recipe times in this book have been worked out for an average oven of 600-650 watts output. But the wattage of your own oven may be as high as 800 or as low as 400 watts. You will have to cut down the cooking times on the higher rated models and increase them on those with a lower output.

Where recipe instructions state HIGH, this is the maximum speed on your oven. MEDIUM indicates 70% of the full power and may be marked MEDIUM or ROAST. LOW indicates 50% power and may also be marked DEFROST, SIMMER or LOW. In addition some ovens have a very low setting for gently thawing or keeping food warm. On a single speed 500 watt oven, increase timings on HIGH, adhere to the timings on MEDIUM and cut the times a little on LOW. Timings on single setting ovens of more than 650 watts should be reduced by a minute or two on HIGH, cut by a quarter on MEDIUM and by half on LOW. It is also helpful to give rest periods of 30 seconds every 2 minutes when adapting LOW instructions to high single setting ovens.

Advice on cooking times is given in the individual chapters, but you will soon recognize the signs just as you do in conventional cooking. It is better to allow too little than too much time, as undercooked food can always be returned to the oven, whereas nothing can put it right if it is overcooked. Many foods continue cooking after removal from the oven and this is indicated in the recipes.

The number of servings is given for each recipe. If you wish to halve the recipe, not only must you halve the ingredients, but the cooking time must also be reduced. Allow one-third of the stated cooking time, test and continue cooking if necessary. As a rule of thumb, HIGH settings are used for poultry, fish, fruit, sauces and soups. MEDIUM is best for egg and cheese dishes, tender meat and sweets. LOW is used for defrosting, egg custards and tough meat.

SOUPS AND APPETIZERS

All types of soup can be prepared in the microwave oven and up to 4 pints can be cooked at one time. Empty canned soup directly into individual bowls, adding an extra tablespoon of water to each. It will only take a minute or two to heat each serving, whether it be in a tureen or individual bowls. The soup is ready when large bubbles form round the edge of the bowl. Stir the soup before serving to distribute the heat evenly.

Dehydrated packet soups should be reconstituted in the serving bowl and brought near to boiling point. Dried soups containing pieces of vegetable such as peas, carrots, rice and noodles should be cooked either on HIGH and then rested a few moments before completing cooking or reduced to LOW.

Home made soups are usually cooked on HIGH and time can be saved by adding only half of the given quantity of liquid during most of the cooking time and the rest just before serving. This is also convenient for freezer storage. Soups can be cooked and frozen with half of the given quantity of liquid. When required, place the frozen soup in a tureen or serving bowl and heat on HIGH until thawed. Stir in the remaining liquid and cook on MEDIUM until the soup is bubbling.

Soup will cook faster if covered and this also prevents splashing when thick soups come to the boil. Home made soups can be cooked in tureens or serving bowls if these are made of china, heat-resistant glass or other microwave proof material. If the dish has no lid, cover loosely with a piece of plastic cling film.

Appetizers and starters are quick to prepare and even quicker to reheat. Pâté or cream cheese piled onto cold toast, dry biscuits or stuffed into bouchées and popped into the microwave oven for a few seconds, are delicious. Prawns, shrimps, snails and oysters can be cooked and dressed in many guises. Hot spiced grapefruit or orange are favourites among the fruit starters and artichokes, palm hearts or asparagus are the best of the vegetables for hors d'oevres.

For a cocktail party or light buffet serve a selection of appetizers. Choose canapés, bouchées, coquilles and other tasty dishes which can be prepared well in advance and heated through in the microwave oven just before serving.

CREAM OF MUSHROOM SOUP (*page 15*)

Courgette (Zucchini) Soup

1½ lb. courgettes (zucchini) washed and trimmed
10 oz. can consommé
½ pint (1¼ cups) water
1 small onion, roughly chopped
2 slices bacon, cooked and crumbled

1 clove garlic, crushed
2 tablespoons (3T) chopped fresh parsley
½ teaspoon dried basil
salt
freshly ground black pepper
fresh Parmesan cheese, grated

Cut the courgettes into 1 inch slices. Place in a large heat resistant casserole. Gradually mix in the remaining ingredients, except the cheese.

Cook, covered on HIGH for 15 minutes or until the courgettes are tender. Stir every 5 minutes during cooking. Cool slightly.

Sieve the soup or emulsify in an electric blender until smooth. Adjust the seasoning, if necessary. Return to the casserole dish. Reheat until the soup reaches boiling point.

Pour the soup into individual bowls and sprinkle a little grated cheese over each serving.
Serves 4-6

French Onion Soup

3 onions, thinly sliced
2 oz. (¼ cup) butter
1¾ pints (4½ cups) beef stock (bouillon)

3 tablespoons (¼ cup) dry red wine
1 teaspoon salt
6 slices French bread, toasted
Parmesan cheese, grated

Place the onions and butter in a large heat resistant bowl. Cook covered on HIGH for 10 minutes. Stir in the stock, wine and salt. Continue cooking for a further 5 minutes. Pour the soup into individual bowls, sprinkle the toast with cheese and float a slice on each serving. Reheat on HIGH for 30 seconds.
Serves 6

Cream of Mushroom Soup

1 oz. (2T) butter, softened
1 oz. (¼ cup) flour
3 chicken stock (bouillon) cubes
¾ pint (2 cups) milk
salt, pepper

4 oz. (1 cup) mushrooms,
  chopped
1½ tablespoons (2T) lemon juice
2 tablespoons (3T) chopped fresh
  parsley

Combine all the ingredients except the lemon juice and parsley, with 1 pint (2½ cups) hot water in a large heat resistant bowl. Cook uncovered on HIGH for 5-6 minutes until boiling. Stir vigorously, then continue cooking on MEDIUM for 10 minutes. Sieve the soup or purée in an electric blender and return to the bowl. Cook on HIGH for about 5 minutes until the soup reaches boiling point. Stir in the lemon juice just before serving. Sprinkle with chopped parsley to garnish. Serve with crusty French bread or wholewheat rolls.

Serves 4-6

For microwave ovens without variable control of 650 watts output or over, cook for 12 minutes before blending, but remember to use a very large bowl and stir frequently.

For a richer flavour, stir 3 tablespoons (¼ cup) single (light) cream into the soup before serving.

Tomato Soup

½ oz. (1T) butter
1 onion, chopped
½ oz. (2T) flour
1 teaspoon Worcestershire sauce
1 tablespoon (1T) lemon juice
1 chicken stock (bouillon) cube

1½ lb. tomatoes, peeled and
  roughly chopped
1 teaspoon dried basil
1 bay leaf
salt, pepper

Put the butter and onion in a large heat resistant bowl and cook for 2 minutes. Blend in the flour and cook for a further 1 minute. Gradually stir in 1¼ pints (3 cups) water, then add the sauce, lemon juice, stock cube, tomatoes, basil, bay leaf, salt and pepper. Cook uncovered on HIGH for 10 minutes.

Remove the bay leaf, sieve the soup or purée in an electric blender then return to the bowl. Cover and continue cooking for a further 5 minutes until the soup is boiling.

Serves 4-6

Gazpacho

1 ¼ pints (3 cups) tomato juice
2 beef stock (bouillon) cubes
2 ripe tomatoes, peeled and
  chopped
1 oz. (¼ cup) green pepper,
  chopped
1 oz. (¼ cup) onion, chopped
3 tablespoons (¼ cup) wine
  vinegar

1 ½ tablespoons (2T) olive oil
1 teaspoon salt
1 clove garlic, crushed
1 teaspoon Worcestershire sauce
few drops Tabasco sauce
Garnish:
chopped tomato, onion and green
  pepper
sliced cucumber

Pour the tomato juice into a 2½ quart heat resistant bowl and cook
uncovered on HIGH for 6 minutes until boiling. Stir in the stock cubes and
chopped tomatoes. Add the green pepper, onion, vinegar, oil, salt, garlic
and sauces and continue cooking for 2 minutes. Serve accompanied by
bowls of chopped vegetables.
Serves 6

Bouillabaisse

2 tablespoons (3T) tomato purée
1 small onion, finely chopped
1 clove garlic, crushed
1 ½ tablespoons (2T) dried parsley
2 ½ teaspoons salt
1 teaspoon lemon juice
¼ teaspoon curry powder

¼ teaspoon pepper
1 lb. fish fillets, cut into 2 inch
  pieces
12 oz. frozen shrimps, thawed
6 oz. frozen crab or lobster meat,
  thawed
1 pint oysters or clams

Combine all the ingredients in a large heat resistant bowl. Add 1¾ pints
(4½ cups) boiling water. Cover and cook on HIGH for about 12 minutes.
Stir, then continue cooking for a further 8-10 minutes until the seafood is
tender. Leave to stand for 5 minutes before serving. Garnish with
croûtons.
Serves 10

Summer Fruit Soup

1¼ lb. frozen raspberries
2 chicken stock (bouillon) cubes
6 tablespoons (½ cup) pineapple
  juice

1 oz. (2T) sugar
6 tablespoons (½ cup) soured
  cream

Put the raspberries in a bowl, cover and cook on HIGH for 1 minute. Stir, then continue cooking for a further 1 or 2 minutes. Stir and leave to stand for 2 minutes until thawed. Purée the raspberries in an electric blender, then press through a nylon sieve into a bowl. Dissolve the stock cubes in ½ pint (1¼ cups) hot water. Combine the stock, pineapple juice and sugar in a large heat resistant bowl.

Stir until the sugar has dissolved. Cook uncovered on HIGH for 2 minutes, then add the raspberry purée. Refrigerate for several hours. Garnish each bowl with a spoonful of soured cream before serving.
Serves 6

Hot Apple Slaw with Ham

4 tablespoons (⅓ cup) vinegar
1 oz. (2T) sugar
1 teaspoon celery seeds
1 teaspoon salt
1 small red dessert apple, washed
  but not peeled

1 lb. (6 cups) cabbage, shredded
1 oz. (2T) butter
8 thin slices ham
4 tomatoes, quartered

Combine the vinegar, sugar, celery seeds, salt and 3 tablespoons (¼ cup) water in a large heat resistant bowl. Cut the apple into quarters, core and thinly slice. Add to the bowl with the shredded cabbage. Dot with butter, cover and cook on HIGH for 4-5 minutes until heated through. Leave to stand, covered, for 3 minutes, then toss. Serve on a platter surrounded by rolled slices of ham and quartered tomatoes.
Serves 4

Oyster Casino

2 dozen oysters, freshly opened
3 slices bacon
1 oz. (¼ cup) seasoned
  breadcrumbs
1 ½ tablespoons (2T) finely
  chopped onion
1 ½ tablespoons (2T) finely
  chopped green pepper

1 ½ tablespoons (2T) finely
  chopped parsley
1 ½ tablespoons (2T) finely
  chopped celery
½ oz. (1T) butter
1 teaspoon Worcestershire sauce
few drops Tabasco sauce
paprika, to garnish

Place 2 oysters in the deep half of one shell. Repeat to fill 12 shells. Arrange on a paper plate. Put the bacon between 2 sheets of absorbent kitchen paper and cook on HIGH for 3 minutes. Chop the bacon and combine with all the remaining ingredients. Spoon over the oysters. Cook on HIGH for 4 minutes. Garnish with a sprinkling of paprika and serve hot.
Serves 4-6

Cocktail Meat Balls

1 ½ lb. lean minced (ground) beef
1 egg, beaten
2 oz. (½ cup) dry breadcrumbs

12 oz. bottle chilli sauce
6 oz. grape jelly
1 ½ tablespoons (2T) lemon juice

Combine the beef, egg and breadcrumbs with 6 tablespoons (½ cup) water in a mixing bowl. Shape into walnut-sized balls. Put the sauce, jelly and lemon juice in a 3 quart heat resistant bowl. Add the meat balls and stir gently. Cook uncovered on HIGH for 12 minutes. Skim off any fat. Stir, then cover and continue cooking for a further 8 minutes until the sauce bubbles and the meat balls are cooked.
Serves 10-12

Escargots

4 oz. (½ cup) butter
1 clove garlic, crushed
1 tablespoon chopped fresh
  parsley
salt, pepper

nutmeg
4½ oz. can snails
24 shells
wine glass of white wine

Combine the butter, garlic and parsley in a heat resistant jug. Cook on HIGH for 1 minute or until the butter bubbles.

Season with salt, pepper and nutmeg. Refrigerate for 1 hour. Put ¼ teaspoon of the mixture into each snail shell. Gently insert the snail and top with more escargot butter.

Arrange the escargots open side up in a heat resistant dish. Pour 1 teaspoon wine over each snail. Cover with plastic cling film. Cook on HIGH for ¾-1 minute until the butter begins to bubble.

Serves 4

Coquilles St. Jacques

1 lb. fresh or frozen scallops
1 lb. mushrooms
2½ oz. (5T) butter
1½ tablespoons (2T) lemon juice
8 fluid oz. (1 cup) dry white wine
¼ teaspoon dried savory
1 bay leaf

½ teaspoon salt
pinch of pepper
¾ oz. (3T) flour
8 fl. oz. (1 cup) single (light) cream
1 oz. (½ cup) fresh breadcrumbs,
  toasted
paprika

Defrost the scallops if frozen. Cut into quarters. Set aside. Wash, drain and slice the mushrooms. Put in a heat resistant bowl with half the butter and the lemon juice. Cook on HIGH for 1 minute. Stir, then cook for a further minute. Drain.

Combine the wine, savory, bay leaf, salt and pepper in a 1½ quart heat resistant dish. Add the scallops. Cook on HIGH for 3 minutes. Drain, reserving a scant ½ pint (1 cup) of the stock. Put the remainder of the butter in a 2 quart heat resistant dish. Cook for ½ minute until melted. Blend in the flour to form a smooth paste. Gradually stir in the stock then the cream. Cook on HIGH for 5-5½ minutes until the sauce thickens. Stir every 30 seconds. Mix the scallops and mushrooms with the sauce and cook on HIGH for 6-7 minutes until thoroughly reheated.

Spoon into scallop shells or ramekins. Garnish with breadcrumbs and paprika just before serving.

Serves 6-8

Hot Roquefort Canapés

3 oz. (½ cup) cream cheese
1 oz. (¼ cup) Roquefort or other
  strong flavoured cheese,
  crumbled

2 oz. (½ cup) walnuts, finely
  chopped
¼ teaspoon dry mustard
½ teaspoon Worcestershire sauce
cracker biscuits or Melba toast

Put the cream cheese in a small heat resistant bowl and cook uncovered on LOW for 30 seconds until the cheese is soft. Add the Roquefort cheese, 1 oz. (¼ cup) walnuts, mustard and sauce and blend well. Spread the mixture on the cracker biscuits. Arrange a maximum of 10 canapés on a large paper plate and cook uncovered on MEDIUM for 1 minute until the cheese begins to melt. Garnish with the remaining walnuts and serve hot.
Makes 20
On ovens without variable control with an output of 650 watts or more, mix all the filling ingredients together and cook for 20 seconds only.

Hot Crab Meat Canapés

6½ oz. can crab meat
6 tablespoons (½ cup)
  mayonnaise
1 teaspoon lemon juice

cayenne pepper
cracker biscuits or Melba toast
paprika

Rinse and drain the crab meat and remove any ligament or shell. Shred the crab meat with a fork. Combine the crab meat, mayonnaise and lemon juice in a bowl. Season to taste with cayenne pepper. Spread about 1 teaspoon of crab mixture on each cracker biscuit and sprinkle with paprika.
  Arrange 2 canapés on a large heat resistant serving platter. Heat on MEDIUM for 2 minutes until heated through. Repeat with the remaining canapés. Serve hot.
Makes 24
For microwave ovens without variable control of 650 watts or greater output, heat each batch for 30 seconds only.

Pâté Maison

1 lb. bacon slices
1½ lb. chicken livers
2 eggs
8 cloves garlic, peeled
1 medium onion, peeled and
  quartered
generous ¼ pint (¾ cup) Cognąc
1 teaspoon thyme or marjoram
1 tablespoon (1T) peppercorns

pinch nutmeg
1 teaspoon whole allspice
2 lb. minced (ground) lean pork
1½ lb. fresh minced (ground) pork
  fat
¾ lb. minced (ground) ham or
  tongue
6 tablespoons (½ cup) dry
  Vermouth

Line two 5 × 9 inch glass loaf dishes crosswise with bacon strips, covering
the bottom and sides and allowing a 1 inch overhang around the sides.
Blend 1 lb. chicken livers, eggs, garlic, onion, Cognąc, herbs and spices
together. Combine the purée with the remaining ingredients. Fill each dish
with a quarter of the pâté mixture, top with a row of whole chicken livers.
Add remaining pâté and cover with ends of bacon strips. Pour ¾ pint (2
cups) water into a large heat resistant dish. Cover the pâté with waxed or
greaseproof paper and stand the pan in the dish. Use a large heat resistant
casserole as a cover and cook on HIGH for 30 minutes. Give the dish a half
turn and cook for a further 20 minutes. Remove dishes from the oven and
cover with a weight placed on a sheet of foil and cool thoroughly. Chill and
remove from the mould before serving.
Serves 40

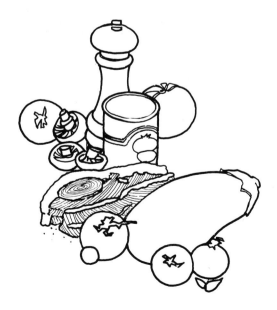

EGG, CHEESE AND LIGHT SUPPER DISHES

Versatile eggs can be cooked in dozens of different ways, either on their own or combined with other ingredients. Egg yolks and egg whites cook at different speeds, so in microwave cookery extra care must be taken to ensure even results. Water will slow cooking down enabling shelled eggs to poach perfectly, provided they are completely immersed. Eggs in their shells will burst if cooked in the microwave oven, but a refrigerated egg may be brought to room temperature if it is put in the microwave oven for not more than 5 seconds. This will lessen the chances of cracking if it is to be soft boiled in boiling water on the hob.

Egg yolks are enclosed in a thin membrane which should be lightly punctured when frying eggs in the microwave oven on HIGH. Ideally MEDIUM is the correct setting and at this speed, puncturing should not be necessary. Fry eggs in a little butter in a pre-heated browning skillet.

Scrambled eggs are lighter and fluffier when cooked in a bowl at HIGH or MEDIUM. Stir frequently and do not overcook. Serve the scrambled eggs as soon as they are set but not dry.

Baked egg custards should be cooked in a dish of boiling water and all such delicately textured dishes will be improved if a glass of water is placed at the back of the oven.

Cheese should never be overcooked as it becomes tough. When it is the main ingredient, preferably cook on MEDIUM or LOW. High setting ovens will require much shorter cooking times and you will find that you can obtain good results if you split the cooking time into three periods, allowing a few seconds rest between each. When cheese is used as a garnish or in a sauce, add it during the final moments of cooking.

Eggs and cheese in composite dishes will produce perfect results, but unfortunately soufflés are only successful when cooked in an oven with variable control.

Rice and pasta often form the basis of light one-course meals. Both should be cooked in the microwave oven in a large volume of boiling salted water. A knob of butter should be dissolved in the water when cooking pasta to prevent the pieces sticking together. Rice will treble its volume when cooked but since it freezes well, any surplus can be stored for reheating at a future time.

WAKE-UP SPECIAL (*page 26*)

Wake-up Special

½ oz. (1T) butter
1 oz. (¼ cup) green pepper,
  chopped
4 eggs
½-10¾ oz. can condensed cream
  of chicken soup

6 slices bacon, cooked and
  crumbled
salt, pepper

Put the butter and green pepper in a 2 quart heat resistant casserole. Cook on HIGH for 30 seconds. Beat the eggs and soup together and blend into the pepper mixture.

Cook uncovered on HIGH for 4½-5 minutes, stirring every 2 minutes. Crumble the bacon on top. Season with salt and pepper to taste. Serve hot.

Serves 6

Store the remaining soup in a jug in the refrigerator or freezer. When mixed with 6 tablespoons (½ cup) milk, then heated on HIGH for 1½-2 minutes, it can be used as a sauce for other egg dishes.

Welsh Rarebit

2 eggs
⅓ pint (1 cup) beer
10 oz. Cheddar cheese, cubed
1 oz. (2T) butter

1 teaspoon dry mustard
1 teaspoon Worcestershire sauce
4 drops Tabasco sauce
4 slices freshly buttered toast

Put the eggs into a 1 quart heat resistant casserole. Beat thoroughly, then stir in the beer, cheese, butter, mustard and sauces. Cook uncovered on HIGH for 5-6 minutes until the cheese has melted and the mixture thickened, stirring once every minute. Beat with a wire whisk until the mixture is smooth. Pile onto the toast and serve at once.

Serves 4

Bacon Omelette with Pimento

8 slices bacon
6 eggs
4 tablespoons (⅓ cup) milk
6 tablespoons (½ cup)
  mayonnaise

1 oz. (¼ cup) pimento, chopped
1 oz. (¼ cup) green pepper,
  chopped
¼ teaspoon salt
tomato slices to garnish

Place the bacon slices between sheets of absorbent kitchen paper in a 1½ quart (10 × 6 inch) heat resistant dish. Cook on HIGH for 7-9 minutes until the bacon is crisp. Drain off any fat, crumble the bacon and set aside. Whisk the eggs, milk and mayonnaise together in a mixing bowl. Add the bacon, pimento, green pepper and salt. Pour into the baking dish. Cover and cook on HIGH for 5-6 minutes until the centre is almost set. Garnish with the tomato slices. Cover and leave to stand for 5 minutes before serving.
Serves 4-6

Egg Florentine

12 oz. leaf spinach
4 eggs

salt, pepper
½ oz. (1T) butter

Put the spinach in a heat resistant serving dish and defrost if frozen. Drain away any excess liquid. Make 4 indentations in the spinach and break an egg carefully into each. Season with salt and pepper and dot with butter. Cover and cook on HIGH for 6-8 minutes until the eggs are cooked. Serve at once.
Serves 2-4

Hot Mexican Rice

4 oz. (1 cup) onion, chopped
1 medium green pepper, diced
1 small chilli pepper, chopped
1 clove garlic, crushed
3½ oz. (½ cup) long grain rice
3 tablespoons (¼ cup) vegetable
  oil
1 lb. minced (ground) beef
16 oz. can tomatoes

4 oz. (¾ cup) seedless raisins
1 oz. (¼ cup) pine nuts
1 tablespoon (1T) chilli powder
2 teaspoons salt
¼ teaspoon pepper
Garnish:
parsley sprigs
2-3 chilli peppers (optional)

Pre-heat the 9½ inch size browning skillet on HIGH for 4½ minutes. Sauté the onion, green pepper, chilli pepper, garlic and rice in the oil on HIGH for 3 minutes. Stir every minute. Mix in the beef and cook uncovered on HIGH for 3 minutes, stirring frequently. Stir in the remaining ingredients. Cover and cook on HIGH for 9-10 minutes until the meat and rice are tender. Leave to stand, covered, for 10 minutes. Fluff with a fork before serving. Garnish with parsley sprigs and whole chilli peppers, if liked.
Serves 4

Rice Pilaf

1 oz. (2T) butter
3½ oz. (½ cup) long grain rice
1½ tablespoons (2T) finely
  chopped onion
1½ tablespoons (2T) finely
  chopped parsley

1½ tablespoons (2T) finely
  chopped celery
4 oz. (1 cup) mushrooms, sliced
1 chicken stock (bouillon) cube

Combine the butter, rice, onion, parsley and celery in a 1 quart heat resistant casserole. Cover and cook on HIGH for 3 minutes until the onion and celery are almost tender.

Add ¼ pint (⅔ cup) water together with the remaining ingredients, cover tightly and cook on LOW for 18 minutes until the rice is almost tender. Stir halfway through the cooking time.

Leave to stand, covered, for 5 minutes to finish cooking. Serve hot.
Serves 2
On ovens without variable control of 650 watts output or over cook the dish for about 12 minutes, stirring occasionally.

Pastry Flan Case

4 oz. (1 cup) flour
½ teaspoon salt
2½ oz. (5T) lard (shortening)

2 tablespoons (3T) ice cold water
yellow food colouring

Sift the flour and salt into a mixing bowl. Cut the fat into the flour using a table knife. Tint the water with a few drops of yellow food colouring and sprinkle over the mixture, a tablespoon at a time, stirring with a fork to form a soft smooth dough. Roll out the pastry to fit a 9 inch flan dish. Trim and flute the edges. Cover with a piece of absorbent kitchen paper and place an 8 inch plate on top. Cook on HIGH for 3 minutes, remove the plate and the paper and continue cooking for a further 1-2 minutes until the pastry is cooked in the centre.

If the desired filling requires cooking, either prepare separately or turn into the baked pastry case and continue cooking by microwave for the amount of time needed to cook the filling. It may be necessary to cover the edges of the pastry with a tiny rim of aluminium foil to prevent overcooking.

Quiche Lorraine

1 cooked 9 inch pastry case (see
  recipe above)
6 slices bacon, cooked and
  crumbled
2 oz. (½ cup) Gruyère cheese,
  grated
3 spring onions (scallions), thinly
  sliced

¼ teaspoon salt
¼ teaspoon nutmeg
pinch of cayenne pepper
1 tablespoon (1½T) flour
¾ pint (2 cups) single (light) cream
4 eggs, lightly beaten
parsley sprigs to garnish
bacon roll, fried (optional)

Prepare the pastry case and leave to cool. Sprinkle the bacon, cheese and onion into the pastry case.

Combine the salt, nutmeg, cayenne and flour in a large heat resistant bowl. Gradually stir in the cream, blending well. Cook on HIGH for 3-4 minutes until bubbling. Stir every 30 seconds.

Slowly stir the hot creamy mixture into the eggs. Pour into the pastry case and cook uncovered on HIGH for 3½-4 minutes. Give the dish a quarter turn every minute. Leave to stand for 5 minutes, then brown under the grill. Garnish with sprigs of parsley and a crisp bacon roll, if liked.
Serves 4-6
It is essential to only half fill pastry cases as quiche fillings rise during cooking and then flatten when cold. Make sure that there are no cracks in the pastry case or the filling will seep through. If necessary, fold a piece of plastic film round the sides and base during cooking in the microwave oven.

Baked Lentils

½ lb. lentils, washed
2 slices bacon, chopped
2 oz. (¼ cup) brown sugar
1 oz. (¼ cup) onion, chopped
3 tablespoons (¼ cup) chilli sauce

3 oz. (¼ cup) black treacle
 (molasses)
1 teaspoon salt
1 teaspoon made mustard

Combine all the ingredients with 1¼ pints (3 cups) water in a 3 quart heat resistant casserole. Cover and cook on HIGH for 10 minutes. Stir, then continue cooking covered on LOW for 50-55 minutes until tender. Leave to stand, covered, for 5 minutes before serving. Water may be added if necessary during cooking time.

Serves 5-6

On microwave ovens without variable control of 650 watts or greater output, cook for 40 minutes, stirring occasionally. The dish will be improved if it is left to stand for 2 minutes four times during the cooking period.

Scotch Woodcock

2 eggs
1 oz. (2T) butter
1 tablespoon (1T) milk
¼ teaspoon salt

pinch of pepper
2 slices freshly buttered toast
4 anchovies
2 teaspoons capers

Combine the eggs, butter, milk, salt and pepper in a heat resistant jug. Cook uncovered on HIGH for 1½-2½ minutes, stirring every 30 seconds. Cut the toast into triangles. Pile the egg mixture on the toast and top with anchovies and capers. Arrange on a paper plate and reheat on HIGH for 30 seconds.

Serves 2

Kedgeree

1 ½ oz. (3T) butter
12 oz. (2 cups) long grain rice,
  cooked
8 oz. smoked haddock, cooked
  and flaked

2 hardboiled eggs, chopped
1 tablespoon (1T) chopped fresh
  parsley

Put the butter in a heat resistant casserole. Heat on HIGH for about 1
minute until melted. Mix in the rice, haddock flakes and chopped eggs.
Cook on HIGH for 3 minutes. Leave for 2 minutes, then fork into a neat
pyramid.
    Garnish with parsley and serve hot.
Serves 3

Spaghetti Carbonara

2 oz. thin spaghetti
½ teaspoon salt
1 teaspoon butter
1 slice bacon, chopped
1 tablespoon (1T) onion, finely
  chopped

1 oz. (3T) Parmesan cheese,
  grated
3 oz. (⅓ cup) cooked ham,
  minced (ground)
¼ teaspoon pepper
fresh parsley to garnish

Combine the spaghetti, ¾ pint (2 cups) boiling water, salt and butter in a
2 quart heat resistant bowl. Cover and cook on HIGH for 7 minutes.
Remove the bowl from the oven and leave to stand, covered, for 5
minutes. Meanwhile combine the bacon and onion in a heat resistant
serving dish. Cook uncovered on HIGH for 3 minutes until the onion is
tender. Drain the spaghetti, add to the onion mixture and stir in the cheese,
ham and pepper.
    Garnish with sprigs of parsley.
Serves 1

Lasagne

1 tablespoon (1T) olive oil
1½ lb. minced (ground) beef
1 clove garlic, crushed
4 tablespoons (⅓ cup) finely
  chopped parsley
1 teaspoon salt
½ teaspoon dried oregano
½ teaspoon dried basil
½ teaspoon sugar
6 oz. can tomato purée

16 oz. can tomatoes
1 lb. cottage cheese
1 egg, lightly beaten
pinch of pepper
12-15 sheets lasagne, cooked
1 lb. Mozzarella cheese, thinly
  sliced
2 oz. (½ cup) Parmesan cheese,
  grated

Put the oil in a large heat resistant bowl and heat on HIGH for 1 minute. Add the beef and cook uncovered on HIGH for 5 minutes until browned. Stir frequently. Drain off the excess fat.

Stir in the garlic, 2 tablespoons (3T) parsley, ½ teaspoon salt, oregano, basil, sugar, tomato purée, tomatoes and 3 tablespoons (¼ cup) water. Cook uncovered on HIGH for 5 minutes.

Combine the cottage cheese, egg, remaining parsley, salt and pepper in a small bowl. Pour just enough of the meat sauce into a 2 quart shallow heat resistant serving dish to cover the bottom. Add a layer of lasagne, then a layer of cottage cheese mixture and a layer of Mozzarella slices. Sprinkle with Parmesan cheese. Continue these layers finishing with a layer of Parmesan cheese. Cook uncovered on HIGH for 10 minutes, giving the dish a half turn after 5 minutes. Leave to stand for 5 minutes before serving.
Serves 6

34

FISH AND SHELLFISH

Fish is no less than superb cooked by microwave. Its moist and delicate texture should not be spoilt by conventional dry heat which may cause the flesh to toughen. In the microwave oven fish can be cooked without the addition of butter or salt, an advantage for those on low salt or low fat diets. Only add liquid if it is to be cooked in a sauce or a court bouillon. Add a sprinkling of lemon juice to soften the bones so providing extra calcium, but leave the salt to seasoning at the table.

Shellfish retain more vitamins cooked in the microwave oven because of the speed of cooking and should be cooked until tender. Never, however, overcook any form of fish or the protein in this highly nutritious food will toughen.

Tuna Cocottes

3 oz. (6T) butter
4 oz. (1 cup) onion, chopped
4 oz. (1 cup) celery, chopped
1 tablespoon (1T) chopped green
  pepper
1½ tablespoons (1T) chopped
  fresh parsley
4 oz. (1 cup) dry breadcrumbs
2 hard boiled eggs, chopped

6 tablespoons (½ cup) double
  (heavy) cream
2 tablespoons (3T) lemon juice
3-7 oz. cans tuna fish, drained
1 teaspoon salt
¼ teaspoon pepper
¼ teaspoon dried oregano
2 eggs, beaten

Put 2 oz. (4T) of the butter in a large heat resistant bowl and cook on HIGH for 1 minute until melted. Stir in the onion, celery, green pepper and parsley and cook for 3 minutes. Add three quarters of the breadcrumbs, the chopped hard boiled eggs, cream and lemon juice. Mix well. Flake the tuna fish, season with salt and pepper, add the oregano and gently fold into the breadcrumb mixture. Bind with the beaten egg. Divide the mixture between 8 individual cocotte dishes. Melt the remaining butter and brush over the tuna moulds, sprinkle the remaining breadcrumbs on top and arrange the cocottes in a circle in the oven. Cook uncovered on HIGH for 12-15 minutes until heated through.

Serve with anchovy sauce, if liked.
Serves 8

Poached Salmon Steaks

4 tablespoons (⅓ cup) dry white
  wine
2 peppercorns
1 bay leaf
1 teaspoon salt
pinch of pepper
1 lemon, thinly sliced
1 tablespoon (1T) dried (instant
  minced) onion
4-5 salmon steaks

Dill and parsley sauce:
6 tablespoons (½ cup) soured
  cream
1 teaspoon lemon juice
1 tablespoon (1T) chopped fresh
  parsley
½ teaspoon dried dill weed
Garnish:
1 lemon, halved
parsley sprigs

Put the wine, peppercorns, bay leaf, salt, pepper, sliced lemon and onion
with a generous ½ pint (1½ cups) hot water in a 7½ × 12 inch heat
resistant dish. Cook uncovered on HIGH for 5 minutes until boiling.
Carefully place the fish in the hot liquid. Cover and cook on HIGH for 1
minute. Turn the fish and cook for a further minute. Leave to stand for 5
minutes. Drain. Combine the cream, lemon juice, parsley and dill weed.
  Serve the salmon steaks on a platter garnished with the lemon halves
and parsley sprigs. Serve the sauce separately.
Serves 4-5

Buttered Smoked Haddock

1 lb. smoked haddock
½ oz. (1T) butter
cayenne pepper

Put the smoked haddock in a heat resistant dish that just fits. Dot with
butter. Cook on HIGH for 3-4 minutes until the flesh flakes easily. Serve
garnished with a sprinkling of cayenne pepper.
Serves 2

Crab in Sherry Cream Sauce

2 oz. (¼ cup) butter
½ oz. (2T) flour
½ teaspoon salt
2 egg yolks

⅔ pint (1½ cups) single (light) cream
3 tablespoons (¼ cup) dry sherry
12 oz. crab, cooked

Put the butter in a large heat resistant bowl. Cook on HIGH for 1-2 minutes until melted. Blend in the flour and salt. Mix the egg yolks and cream in a small bowl. Stir into the flour mixture to form a smooth paste. Add the sherry and crab. Cover and cook on HIGH for 5 minutes. Stir, then continue cooking for about 5 minutes until the mixture thickens. Leave to stand covered for 5 minutes before serving.

Serve on toast, in bouchées or with cooked rice.
Serves 6

Scampi

1 lb. fresh scampi (jumbo shrimp)
4 oz. (½ cup) butter
1½ tablespoons (2T) lemon juice
1½ tablespoons (2T) dried parsley

1-2 cloves garlic, crushed
½ teaspoon salt
paprika (optional)

Under cold running water, remove the shells from the scampi, leaving the last tail section attached. Using a sharp knife, make a shallow cut lengthwise down the back of each scampi and wash out the sand vein. If desired, the scampi may be butterflied (make a deep cut down the back to remove the sand vein). Put the butter, lemon juice, parsley, garlic to taste and salt in a shallow heat resistant dish.

Cook uncovered on HIGH for 2 minutes. Add the scampi and stir to coat well. If desired, sprinkle with paprika. Cook uncovered for a further 4-6 minutes until the scampi are pink and tender. Stir occasionally. Serve in individual glasses or scallop shells.

Do not overcook scampi or they will become tough.
Serves 4
If desired, lobster, scallops, crab meat or any combination of these may be substituted for scampi.

Frozen seafood may also be used, but the result may be more watery. Allow slightly longer cooking times.

Fillets of Sole with Almonds

2 oz. (¼ cup) butter
1 oz. (¼ cup) flaked almonds
2-8 oz. Dover soles, gutted and
  skinned

2 teaspoons lemon juice
¼ teaspoon salt

Place the butter and almonds in a shallow heat resistant dish. Cook on
HIGH for about 5 minutes until golden, stirring after 2½ minutes.
    Remove the almonds and set aside. Arrange the fish side by side in the
dish. Sprinkle with lemon juice and salt. Turn the fish occasionally to baste.
Cover with plastic cling film and cook on HIGH for 4-5 minutes until the
flesh is white and opaque. Leave to stand covered for 3 minutes before
serving. Garnish with the almonds.
Serves 2

French Fish Fillets

1 lb. fish fillets
3 tablespoons (¼ cup) French
  dressing

1½ oz. (½ cup) matzo meal
  (cracker) crumbs
paprika

Dip the fillets in the French dressing. Coat with the crumbs. Arrange in a
heat resistant buttered dish and sprinkle with paprika. Cook on HIGH for
5-6 minutes, giving the dish a half turn after 3 minutes.
Serves 4

Salmon Stuffed Green Pepper

4 large green peppers
1 lb. can salmon, drained and
  flaked
2 oz. (1 cup) fresh breadcrumbs
2 oz. (½ cup) celery, finely diced
4 tablespoons (⅓ cup)
  mayonnaise
1 egg
1½ tablespoons (2T) lemon juice

1½ tablespoons (2T) prepared
  mustard
1 oz. (2T) butter, softened
1 tablespoon (1T) minced onion
¼ teaspoon salt
few drops Tabasco sauce
2 slices processed cheese, cut into
  strips
parsley sprigs to garnish

Cut a slice from the upper third of each pepper to make a scalloped edge. Finely dice the slices. Remove the seeds and pith from the peppers. Parboil in a few spoonfuls of boiling salted water on HIGH for 4-5 minutes. Drain. Thoroughly mix the diced green peppers with all the remaining ingredients except the cheese. Fill the pepper shells with the salmon mixture.

Place the stuffed peppers upright in a shallow buttered heat resistant dish. Cook on HIGH for 10-12 minutes, giving the dish a quarter turn every 4 minutes.

Arrange the cheese strips on each pepper. Garnish with parsley sprigs and serve with lemon wedges and French fried potatoes, if liked.
Serves 4

Steamed Lobster

½ teaspoon salt
1 lemon, sliced

2-1 lb. live lobsters, pegged
sprigs of parsley, to garnish

Put 6 tablespoons (½ cup) water, salt and lemon in a 3 quart heat resistant casserole. Heat uncovered on HIGH for 2-3½ minutes until the water boils. Place the live lobsters head first into the boiling water. Cover and cook on HIGH for 12 minutes. Leave to stand covered in the oven for 4 minutes to finish cooking. Drain. With a sharp knife split the tail and if the meat is still translucent in the centre, cook covered for a further minute until the meat is opaque. Continue to cut up the centre towards the head. Remove the stomach and intestinal tract. The green liver and the red roe are considered to be delicacies. Lift the lobster on to a serving platter. Garnish with parsley sprigs.

Serve the lobster with Wilted Spinach Salad (see page 63) and rice salad.
Serves 2

Mackerel in Cider

2 small mackerel, gutted and
  cleaned
1 tablespoon (1T) chopped onion
1 tablespoon (1T) chopped fresh
  parsley

½ pint (1 ¼ cups) cider
1 tablespoon (1T) lemon juice
salt, pepper
1 teaspoon butter
1 teaspoon flour

Place the mackerel side by side in a heat resistant casserole.

Mix the onion, parsley, cider, lemon juice, salt and pepper together and pour over the fish. Cook on HIGH for 6 minutes, giving the dish a quarter turn every 1½ minutes. Lift the mackerel onto a serving dish and cover. Strain the liquor into a heat resistant bowl.

Blend the butter and flour together and form into a ball. Stir into the liquor.

Cook for 1-2 minutes, stirring every 30 seconds until the sauce thickens. Pour the sauce over the mackerel and serve at once.

Serves 2

Baked Salmon

4-4 oz. salmon steaks
2 oz. (¼ cup) butter
salt, pepper

1 tablespoon (1T) lemon juice
parsley to garnish

Arrange the salmon in a shallow square heat resistant dish with the thicker parts of the steaks towards the outside. Dot with butter, season with salt and pepper and add a sprinkling of lemon juice. Cover with a sheet of waxed or greaseproof paper.

Cook on HIGH for 6-8 minutes, turning the fish after 3 minutes. Leave to stand for 5 minutes before testing. The steaks are cooked when the bone separates easily from the flesh. Garnish with sprigs of parsley.

Serves 4

Frozen salmon steaks should be thawed before cooking to prevent the flesh from toughening.

Poached Sole
with Shrimp Sauce

1½ lb. frozen sole or plaice fillets
1½ tablespoons (2T) chopped
  shallots
salt, pepper
⅓ pint (¾ cup) dry white wine
2 oz. (4T) butter

½ oz. (2T) flour
8 fl. oz. (1 cup) single (light) cream
  or milk
4½ oz. can medium sized shrimps,
  rinsed and drained
chopped fresh parsley to garnish

Put the frozen fish fillets in a shallow buttered heat resistant dish. Cook, covered, on HIGH for 2 minutes. Separate the fillets. Re-arrange evenly in the dish and sprinkle with the shallots, salt and pepper to taste. Pour the wine over the fish.

Cook, covered, on HIGH for 10 minutes until the fish flakes easily. Baste several times during cooking. Lift the fish gently onto a heat resistant serving dish and set aside leaving the liquor in the original dish.

Put the butter in a small heat resistant bowl and heat for 30 seconds until melted. Blend in the flour, then add the cream, mixing well. Cook uncovered on MEDIUM for 4-5 minutes until thickened and smooth. Stir occasionally. Set the sauce aside.

Heat the fish liquor uncovered in the dish on MEDIUM for 4-6 minutes until it has reduced to about 6 tablespoons (½ cup). Add the cream sauce and the shrimps and stir until well blended. Spoon over the fish, then reheat uncovered on MEDIUM for 2-3 minutes until heated through. Garnish with chopped parsley.

Serves 4

On microwave ovens without variable control with an output of 650 watts or over great care must be taken to avoid curdling the sauce. The cream sauce should be heated for only 20 seconds, then stirred and the process repeated until the sauce is thick.

Cook the fish liquor for about 3 minutes. Reheat the fish for 1 minute before cooking with the sauce.

MEAT AND POULTRY

Tender cuts of meat cook well in the microwave oven. Tougher cheaper cuts which conventionally would be used in casseroles and stews, must first be tenderized to help break down the fibres. High speed microwave ovens should be used for chops and steaks in conjunction with either the built-in grill or the browning skillet. At this speed tougher cuts must be marinated or minced, but will cook successfully on LOW in ovens with variable control.

Meat should be cut into even sized pieces and stirred occasionally during cooking. Microwaves cook mostly round the outside of the plate, so arrange chops or larger pieces of meat with the thinner parts towards the centre. Microwaves cook through the outer 2 inches simultaneously and the inner meat is cooked by conduction — the effect of each heat layer on its cooler neighbour, so that any food more than 4 inches in diameter will take longer to cook. Joints of beef which may be required rare are therefore easy to cook in a microwave oven. Brown the joint after cooking under a hot grill or use the built-in grill if your oven has one.

Poultry weighing up to 3 lb. or pieces of chicken will cook evenly, but larger birds should have either rest periods or a lowering of the cooking speed to ensure they cook through.

Heat is retained in large pieces of meat, so that joints and whole poultry should be left to rest for several minutes to allow the heat to redistribute before carving.

The microwave oven is frequently used for defrosting. Many foods can be thawed and reheated or cooked in one sequence. Both meat and chicken should be thawed before cooking unless they are first cut into very thin pieces. Use the guide given in the oven handbook as defrosting systems vary. Generally speaking defrost large joints on a medium setting and small joints on a low setting. Meat should be removed from the oven while the centre is still frozen and a standing time allowed for the internal temperature to become even. A 3 lb. joint will take approximately 30 minutes on LOW plus a standing time of up to 1 hour. A larger joint will take 20-25 minutes and require a standing time of up to 2 hours.

Similar rules apply to poultry but remember to remove the giblets from a frozen bird and cook them separately. A standing time is not usually necessary, a short soak in cold water will complete defrosting if any large crystals remain in the cavity.

On ovens without variable control of over 650 watts output cook for 1 minute per pound of frozen meat or poultry and leave to stand for 10 minutes. Repeat as necessary. You will find that the total time from freezer to table is the same whichever method of microwave thawing is used.

44 ROAST STUFFED CHICKEN (*page 47*)

Perfect Meat Roasts

Place the roast fat side down on an upturned saucer or microwave grill in a heat resistant baking dish. Cook uncovered for half the cooking time.

Drain the pan juices and reserve if gravy is to be made. Turn the meat over, cover loosely with waxed or greaseproof paper and complete cooking according to the roasting chart.

Cover the meat with aluminium foil and leave to stand for 15 to 30 minutes until the required internal temperature is reached. If necessary remove the aluminium foil and continue cooking for a few more minutes.

Add salt to the meat after cooking and brown under the grill on all sides before lifting on to the serving platter.

Joints are left to stand before serving to allow the heat to distribute evenly. This also helps to prevent the meat juices from oozing out.

Guide to Roasting Times for Meat and Poultry

	Ovens with variable control		Ovens without variable control	Internal temperature after
	minutes per lb. for total cooking period	recommended settings for each half of the cooking period	minutes per lb. for total cooking period	standing time (Fahrenheit)
Beef Rare	9-10	1. High 2. Medium or Low	6-7	140°
Medium	11-12	1. High 2. Medium or Low	7-8	160°
Well done	12-14	1. High 2. Medium or Low	8½-9	170°
Lamb Well done	10-12 or	Medium throughout	8-10	180°
without bone	12-13	Low throughout		
with bone	9-11 or	Medium throughout	7-9	180°
	11-12	Low throughout		
Pork	11-12	1. High 2. Medium or Low	9-10	170°
Veal	18-20 or	Medium throughout	8½-9	170°
	21-22	Low throughout		
Chicken	8-10	1. High 2. Medium or Low	6-8	190°
Duck	8-10	1. High 2. Medium or Low	6-8	190°
Turkey	9-10	1. High 2. Medium or Low	7-9	190°

Roast Stuffed Chicken

1-6 lb. roasting chicken
2 oz. (4T) butter
2 oz. (½ cup) onion, finely
  chopped
2 oz. (½ cup) celery, finely
  chopped
salt, pepper
½ teaspoon caraway seeds
  (optional)
1 chicken stock (bouillon) cube,
  crumbled

12 oz. (3 cups) cubed, day old rye
  bread
¼ oz. (¼ cup) parsley, finely
  chopped
3 tablespoons (¼ cup) honey
1 teaspoon Worcestershire sauce
1 teaspoon soy sauce
parsley sprigs to garnish

Wash the chicken, pat dry with absorbent kitchen paper and set aside. Put the butter in a deep 2 quart heat resistant casserole and heat on HIGH for 30 seconds until melted. Add the onion and celery and cook uncovered on HIGH for about 4 minutes until the vegetables are tender.

Stir in ½ teaspoon salt, ¼ teaspoon pepper, caraway seeds, chicken stock cube, bread and parsley and mix well. Moisten with 3 tablespoons (¼ cup) boiling water, adding a little more if necessary.

Rub the inside of the capon with salt and pepper to taste and put the stuffing in the cavity. Close the cavity with wooden skewers or sew with string. Combine the honey and sauces and coat the chicken with this mixture.

Put the chicken, breast side up, on an upturned saucer in a shallow heat resistant baking dish. Cook uncovered on MEDIUM for about 48 minutes until a meat thermometer inserted in the thickest part of the bird (not touching any bones) registers 170°F, 75°C. Wrap in aluminium foil and leave to stand for 15 minutes before carving.

Be sure to use a meat thermometer for testing and do not leave it in the oven unless your model has one built in.

Should it be necessary to reheat the chicken, remember to remove all the aluminium foil wrapping first. Garnish with parsley before serving.

Serves 6

On microwave ovens without variable control with an output of 650 watts or more cook uncovered for 20 minutes, then turn the chicken breast down, drain off the surplus fat and continue cooking for a further 20 minutes.

Test with the thermometer, then leave to stand for 15 minutes before carving. The temperature will rise another 10° during this time.

Beef Strogonoff

1 lb. rump steak (tenderloin)
¾ oz. (3T) flour
1½ teaspoons salt
¼ teaspoon pepper
1 clove garlic
3 tablespoons (¼ cup) salad oil
1 oz. (¼ cup) onion, chopped

4 oz. (1 cup) mushrooms, sliced
generous ¼ pint (¾ cup) soured
  cream
2 tablespoons (3T) brandy
1 tablespoon (1T) chopped fresh
  parsley

Trim any excess fat from the meat. Combine the flour, salt and pepper.
Rub both sides of the meat with the garlic clove. Toss the steak in the
seasoned flour.

Cut the beef into strips 1½ × 1 inch. Pre-heat the browning skillet for
4½ minutes. Put the oil and meat into the skillet and stir rapidly to brown
the meat on all sides. Stir in the onion. Cook uncovered on HIGH for 3
minutes. Mix in 3 tablespoons (¼ cup) water and the mushrooms and
continue cooking uncovered for a further 4-5 minutes until the beef is just
tender.

Stir in the soured cream and brandy. Heat for 1 minute. Garnish with
chopped parsley. Serve immediately with buttered noodles or rice.
Serves 3-4

Sweet and Sour Pork

1½ lb. pork, cubed
1½ tablespoons (2T) cornflour
  (cornstarch)
2 tablespoons (3T) soy sauce
2 oz. (¼ cup) brown sugar
¼ teaspoon ground ginger

3 tablespoons (¼ cup) vinegar
13¼ oz. can pineapple tidbits,
  undrained
1 small onion, sliced
2 medium green peppers, cut into
  strips

Toss the pork with the cornflour in a 2 quart heat resistant casserole. Mix in
all the remaining ingredients except the green peppers. Add 6 tablespoons
(½ cup) water. Cover and cook on HIGH for 12 minutes until the pork is
cooked.

Stir once during cooking. Add the green peppers and continue cooking
on HIGH for 1 minute.
Serves 4-6

Chicken à la King

1 ½ oz. (3T) butter
1 ¼ oz. (5T) flour
1 teaspoon salt
pinch of pepper
⅔ pint (1 ¾ cups) chicken stock
  (bouillon)

1 ½ lb. (3 cups) cooked chicken,
  cubed
4 oz. can mushrooms, drained
1 oz. (¼ cup) pimento, chopped
8 medium vol-au-vent cases (puff
  pastry shells), cooked

Put the butter in a deep 2 quart heat resistant bowl. Blend in the flour, salt and pepper. Gradually stir in the chicken stock. Cook uncovered on HIGH for 4 minutes until thickened and smooth. Stir occasionally. Add the remaining ingredients except the pastry cases and cook uncovered on HIGH for 3 minutes until heated through.

Put the pastry cases on a paper platter and heat on HIGH for 2 minutes until warm. Fill each with some of the chicken mixture.

Serve with a mixed salad tossed in French dressing.
Serves 8

Chicken Kebabs

2 lb. boned chicken breasts
4 tablespoons (⅓ cup) soy sauce
½ oz. (1T) sugar
1 teaspoon salt
pinch of pepper
¼ teaspoon ground ginger

¼ teaspoon garlic powder
2 green peppers, cut into ½ inch
  cubes
8 oz. can mushrooms, drained
2 tablespoons (3T) honey

Remove the skin from the chicken breasts and cut the flesh into 1 inch cubes. Combine the soy sauce, sugar, salt, pepper, ginger and garlic powder in a large bowl. Mix thoroughly.

Add the chicken and toss gently to coat the pieces well. Thread the chicken, peppers and mushroom caps alternately on to wooden skewers. Stir the honey into the remaining liquid and brush each kebab liberally with the mixture.

Arrange the kebabs in a single layer in a shallow heat resistant baking dish and cook covered on HIGH for 5-7 minutes until the chicken is cooked and the green peppers tender. Turn the kebabs occasionally during cooking.

Serve hot or cold.
Serves 4-5

Duckling with Orange Sauce

4½-5 lb. duckling
1 teaspoon salt
2 oranges, peeled and quartered
1 clove garlic, crushed
3 peppercorns
2 oz. (¼ cup) unsalted butter
1 oz. (2T) brown sugar
1 tablespoon (1T) cornflour
 (cornstarch)

1 tablespoon (1T) grated orange
 peel
¼ pint (⅔ cup) orange juice
2 tablespoons (3T) duck dripping
2 tablespoons (3T) Curaçao or
 Cointreau

Wash the duckling and set aside the giblets. Fasten the neck skin with wooden skewers. Sprinkle the inside of the cavity with salt. Stuff with oranges, garlic and peppercorns. Close the cavity securely with wooden skewers or tie up with string.

Tie the legs together and the wings to the body. Cover the ends of legs, tail and wings with small pieces of foil.

Place two upturned saucers or a microwave roasting rack in a 2 quart (12 × 7 inch) heat resistant baking dish. Put the duck, breast side down, on the saucers. Cook uncovered on HIGH for 25 minutes. Remove the duck. Drain the juice, remove the foil pieces and replace the duck, breast side up, on the saucers.

Cook on LOW for 25 minutes until cooked, covering if necessary with a sheet of waxed or greaseproof paper to prevent splashing.

Spread the skin with butter and cook uncovered on HIGH for 4 minutes or crispen under a hot grill.

Leave to stand while preparing the sauce. Combine the sugar, cornflour, orange peel, juice and dripping in a large heat resistant measuring jug. Cook on HIGH for 3-4 minutes until the mixture boils and thickens. Stir occasionally. Mix in the liqueur.

Serve the duck cut into quarters or sliced with the orange sauce spooned over each portion.

Serves 4

For microwave ovens without variable control with an output of 650 watts or more, follow the cooking times given in the recipe, but cut down on the second cooking period to 20 minutes. Leave to stand for 15-20 minutes before serving.

Crown Roast of Lamb

4-5 lb. crown roast prepared from
  2 joints of best end neck of lamb
4 oz. (½ cup) butter
2 oz. (½ cup) onion, finely
  chopped
2 oz. (½ cup) celery, finely
  chopped
2 teaspoons lemon juice

1 teaspoon grated orange rind
1 teaspoon salt
¼ teaspoon pepper
1 teaspoon dried sage
pinch of garlic powder
6 oz. (3 cups) fresh white
  breadcrumbs
1 egg, beaten

Remove any lean trimmings from the lamb. Finely mince the trimmings and cook in a heat resistant bowl on HIGH for a few minutes.

Put the butter in a small heat resistant bowl and heat on HIGH for 1 minute until melted. Add the onion and celery and cook uncovered on HIGH for 4 minutes until the vegetables are tender.

Stir in the lemon juice, orange rind, salt, pepper, sage and garlic powder. Add the vegetable mixture and breadcrumbs to the cooked lamb and mix well. Bind the mixture with the beaten egg. Arrange the roast in a shallow heat resistant baking dish.

Spoon the stuffing into the centre of the roast. Cook uncovered on HIGH for 25 minutes until a meat thermometer inserted between two ribs registers 165°F, 75°C. Turn the dish twice during cooking.

Cover the crown roast with aluminium foil and leave to stand at room temperature for 20-30 minutes until the internal temperature reaches 180°F, 80°C. Remove the foil and continue cooking for a few more minutes. Top each bone with a paper frill. Serve with new potatoes and carrots.
Serves 8

Blanquette of Veal

½ lb. boneless veal (shoulder or
  breast), cut into 1 inch cubes
1 oz. (½ cup) button onions,
  peeled
1 carrot, peeled and cut into
  ½ inch slices

bouquet garni
1 teaspoon butter, softened
2 teaspoons flour
3 tablespoons (¼ cup) single
  (light) cream
salt, pepper

Combine the veal, ⅓ pint (¾ cup) water, onions, carrot and bouquet garni in a large heat resistant bowl. Cook covered on HIGH for 20 minutes. Skim. Remove bouquet garni, stir and continue cooking on HIGH for 8 minutes. Transfer the meat and vegetables to a serving dish.

Blend the butter and flour together, add to the liquid and cook uncovered on HIGH for 4 minutes until the sauce has thickened. Stir every minute. Add cream, salt and pepper and pour the sauce over the meat.
Serves 2

CROWN ROAST OF LAMB (*Photograph: New Zealand Lamb
Information Bureau*)

Barbecued Spare Ribs

1½-2 lb. spare ribs (country style)
3 tablespoons (¼ cup) tomato
  ketchup (catsup)
3 tablespoons (¼ cup) chilli sauce
½ oz. (1T) brown sugar
1½ tablespoons (2T) onion,
  chopped

½ teaspoon salt
pinch of garlic powder
1 teaspoon dry mustard
2 teaspoons soy sauce
few drops of Tabasco sauce
1 teaspoon lemon juice

Separate the ribs and arrange in a 2 quart (8 × 8 inch) heat resistant dish, putting the larger pieces round the edge. Cover and cook on HIGH for 12 minutes until partially cooked.

Rearrange the ribs halfway through the cooking time.

Meanwhile combine all the remaining ingredients in a ½ pint (1 cup) glass measuring jug. Remove the ribs from the oven and drain.

Cook the sauce uncovered on HIGH for 1-1½ minutes until the mixture boils. Stir once during cooking.

Dip each rib in the sauce to coat. Cool and refrigerate until ready to grill or fry.

Barbecue over hot coals for 15-20 minutes, turning occasionally until the ribs are browned and heated through.

Serves 3-4

Spare ribs may also be cooked in a preheated browning skillet.

Chicken in Tarragon Sauce

1½ lb. chicken joints, fresh or
  frozen
1 oz. (2T) butter
10 oz. can condensed chicken
  soup

¼ pint (⅔ cup) white wine
½ teaspoon dried tarragon
salt, pepper
8-10 button mushrooms, cooked

Thaw the chicken joints if frozen. Put the butter in a shallow heat resistant serving dish. Heat on HIGH for 30 seconds until melted. Arrange the chicken joints in the dish, turn to coat with the butter, then cover and cook on HIGH for 5 minutes.

Turn the chicken joints again and continue cooking covered for a further 4-5 minutes.

Mix the soup, wine and ½ pint (1¼ cups) water together and pour over the chicken. Sprinkle with tarragon, salt and pepper.

Cover and continue cooking on HIGH for 10 minutes.

Serve garnished with the whole mushrooms.

Serves 3

Swedish Meat Balls

2 oz. (¼ cup) butter
4 oz. (1 cup) onion, finely
  chopped
3 eggs
⅔ pint (1½ cups) milk
1½ teaspoons ground allspice
½ teaspoon ground nutmeg
1 tablespoon (1T) salt

4 oz. (2 cups) fresh breadcrumbs
2 lb. lean minced (ground) beef
1 lb. lean minced (ground) lamb
1 beef stock (bouillon) cube,
  crumbled
1 oz. (4T) flour
¾ pint (2 cups) single (light) cream
  or milk

Put the butter in a large heat resistant bowl and heat on HIGH for 30 seconds until melted. Add the onion and cook uncovered on HIGH for 3 minutes until lightly browned. Set aside.

Beat the eggs and milk together and add to the onions with the allspice, nutmeg, salt and breadcrumbs. Stir, then add the meat and mix well. Form into 1 inch balls and arrange half in a single layer in a shallow 1 quart heat resistant baking dish. Cook on MEDIUM for 7-8 minutes until almost done. Turn the meat balls occasionally during cooking. Remove the cooked meat balls. Cook the remaining meat balls and while these are cooking, dissolve the beef cube in 8 fl. oz. (1 cup) boiling water.

Skim the fat from the cooking dish and mix the remaining meat juices with the stock. Stir in the flour. Cook uncovered on HIGH for 2 minutes until slightly thickened. Stir every 30 seconds.

Gradually stir in the cream and cook on MEDIUM for 8 minutes until thickened and smooth. Stir occasionally.

Return the meat balls to the sauce and reheat on MEDIUM for 1-2 minutes until hot.

Serves 12

For microwave ovens without variable control of 650 watts output or more, cook each batch of meat balls for 4-5 minutes. To avoid curdling, take great care when the cream is added. Cook for 20 seconds. Stir and rest for 5 seconds, then repeat until the sauce is thick, about 4 minutes.

VEGETABLES

Vegetables cooked by microwave look better, taste better and excel those cooked by any other method. All the colour is retained, so that they are pleasing to the eye. The speed of cooking in a minimal amount of water reduces the vitamin loss and there is little chance of overcooking resulting in tasteless vegetables. Microwaved vegetables retain their shape and may be cooked whole, sliced or shredded. Individual preferences can be accommodated, since the oven can be switched off at any point during the cooking period, allowing portions of food to be cooked according to taste.

Vegetables enclosed in skin such as potatoes and peppers, must be pricked or scored to prevent bursting, but then may be cooked whole on the oven shelf. Tomatoes, which have a high moisture content, should be halved before cooking.

With the exception of fresh leeks and frozen chopped spinach, which need no additional moisture, cook sliced vegetables with 4-6 tablespoons water, adding the salt to the water. Vegetables should be covered with a lid or plastic film to retain the moisture — the trapped steam will accelerate cooking.

Little extra cooking time will be required for frozen vegetables, as they will have been partially softened in pre-freeze blanching. Stir vegetables occasionally during cooking to distribute the heat or give a good shake if covered with plastic film. If you are pre-cooking vegetables for serving several hours later, remember to undercook slightly. Always avoid overcooking vegetables, particularly whole runner or French beans, cabbage and jacket potatoes, as this causes the vegetables to become dry.

Most vegetables can be cooked on a HIGH setting. Sauces should be cooked separately and poured over the vegetable, then the whole dish can be reheated.

Sweet and Sour Red Cabbage

1 lb. red cabbage, shredded
2 dessert apples, chopped
1½ tablespoons (2T) cider vinegar
½ oz. (1T) butter

1½ oz. (3T) brown sugar
1 teaspoon salt
1 teaspoon caraway seeds
2-3 cloves (optional)

Combine all the ingredients with a generous ¼ pint (¾ cup) boiling water in a large heat resistant casserole.

Cover and cook on HIGH for 15 minutes, stirring occasionally, until the cabbage is just tender.
Serves 4-6

Creamed Beetroot

1 lb. cooked beetroot, peeled and
 sliced
3 tablespoons (4T) soured cream
1 tablespoon (1T) lemon juice

1 teaspoon sugar
salt, pepper
1 tablespoon (1T) chopped chives

Layer the beetroot in a heat resistant serving dish.
 Combine the cream, lemon juice, and sugar. Add salt and pepper to
taste. Pour over the beetroot and cook on HIGH for 2-3 minutes until
heated through, then sprinkle with the chives and serve at once.
Serves 3-4

Green Peas Française

1 oz. (2T) butter
1 lettuce heart, shredded

10 oz. (2cups) frozen peas
salt, pepper

Combine the ingredients in a 1 quart heat resistant casserole. Cover and
cook for 2 minutes. Stir, then continue cooking for a further 2 minutes.
Serves 3-4

Celery with Tomato Sauce

7 oz. can celery hearts
1 ½ teaspoons brown sugar
1 teaspoon dried oregano

5 tablespoons (6T) tomato
 ketchup (catsup)
2 oz. (½ cup) cheese, grated

Drain the celery hearts and arrange in a shallow heatproof dish. Combine
the sugar, oregano and ketchup. Spread the sauce over the celery and
sprinkle with grated cheese. Cook on HIGH for 3 minutes. Brown under
the grill if desired.
Serves 2

Baked Marrow

1 medium (1 lb.) marrow (squash)   *1 oz. (2T) butter*
1 oz. (2T) brown sugar

Prick the marrow well with a fork. Wrap in a piece of absorbent kitchen paper and cook on HIGH for 6-8 minutes until just tender.

Cut in half lengthwise and remove the seeds. Sprinkle sugar over the cut surfaces and dot with butter. Join the two halves of the marrow together with a wooden cocktail stick at either end and cook for a further 2-3 minutes until the sugar has melted.

Serves 3-4

Baked Potato Boats

4 large potatoes   *2 oz. (½ cup) strong cheese,*
1 oz. (2T) butter   *grated*
8 fl. oz. (1 cup) milk   *paprika*
salt, pepper

Scrub the potatoes and prick thoroughly all the way through with a large fork. Cook on HIGH, arranged in a circle on a piece of absorbent kitchen paper for 16-19 minutes. Turn over halfway through the cooking time. Leave to stand for a few minutes.

Cut a thin slice from the top of each potato. Scrape out the inside, leaving a thin unbroken shell for each potato. Mash the potatoes. Stir in the butter, milk, salt and pepper and whip until the mixture is light and fluffy. Spoon the potato mixture back into the shells. Top each potato with cheese and sprinkle with paprika. Arrange the potatoes in a circle on a paper plate and cook on HIGH for 5 minutes.

Serves 4

Stuffed potatoes may be prepared ahead and refrigerated if desired. Reheat on HIGH for 6-7 minutes.

Ratatouille

2 aubergines (eggplant), cut into
  ½ inch cubes
1 lb. courgettes (zucchini), thinly
  sliced
3 tablespoons (¼ cup) olive oil
2 onions, thinly sliced
1 clove garlic, crushed
1 large green pepper, sliced

3 large ripe tomatoes, each cut
  into 8 wedges
2 teaspoons dried basil
2 teaspoons dried marjoram
1 teaspoon salt
½ teaspoon pepper
8 oz. (2 cups) mushrooms, sliced

Soak the aubergines and courgettes in cold salted water (1 teaspoon salt to 1 quart water) for 30 minutes. Drain. Combine the olive oil, onions and garlic in a large heat resistant bowl and cook uncovered on HIGH for 5 minutes until the onions are tender. Add the green pepper, aubergines and courgettes. Mix well, cover and cook for 5 minutes. Add all the remaining ingredients and continue cooking for a further 5-8 minutes until the vegetables are tender. Serve hot or cold.
Serves 6-8

Broccoli in Lemon Sauce

2-10 oz. packages frozen broccoli
  spears
1 oz. (2T) butter
1 tablespoon (1T) flour
6 tablespoons (½ cup) milk

1 teaspoon grated lemon peel
1 tablespoon (1T) lemon juice
¼ teaspoon salt
¼ teaspoon ground ginger

Arrange the broccoli in a 1½ quart shallow heat resistant dish. Cook covered on HIGH for 14-16 minutes. Drain and set aside. Put the butter in a medium sized heat resistant bowl and heat on HIGH for 30 seconds until melted. Blend in the flour, then gradually stir in the milk. Cook uncovered on MEDIUM for 2-3 minutes until thickened and smooth. Stir in the lemon peel and juice gradually to avoid curdling, then add the salt and ginger. Spoon the sauce over the broccoli spears and reheat uncovered on MEDIUM for 2-3 minutes until heated through.
Serves 4-6
For ovens without variable control of or more than 650 watts output, cook the sauce for 1½-2 minutes, stirring frequently. Reheat the dish for 1 minute only.

Cucumber Ragoût

2 oz. (½ cup) mushrooms,
  chopped
½ oz. (1 T) butter
½ oz. (2 T) cornflour (cornstarch)

¼ pint (⅔ cup) milk
salt, pepper
8 oz. piece of cucumber

Put the mushrooms and butter in a large heat resistant bowl.
   Cook on HIGH for 3 minutes. Blend in the cornflour, then gradually stir in the milk, salt and pepper. Continue cooking for 3 minutes, stirring every minute. Peel and slice the cucumber and arrange in a shallow serving dish. Pour the sauce over the top. Heat for 1 minute.
Serves 2

Fried Mushrooms

4 oz. (½ cup) butter
12 large (morel) mushrooms
2 eggs, beaten well

2½ oz. (1 cup) matzo (cracker)
  meal

Preheat the browning skillet on HIGH for 2½ minutes. Add the butter and heat for 1 minute until melted. Dip the mushrooms in the egg and then the meal, shaking off any loose crumbs. Fry on HIGH for 2-3 minutes until golden brown. Turn the mushrooms over halfway through the cooking time. Drain and serve hot.
Serves 4

Cauliflower Polonaise

1 medium cauliflower
generous ¼ pint (¾ cup) cheese
  sauce, see page 82
2 tablespoons (3 T) fresh
  breadcrumbs

2 oz. (¼ cup) cooked ham,
  chopped

Separate the cauliflower into florets and arrange them in a heat resistant bowl, so that they resemble a whole cauliflower upside down. Add 6 tablespoons (½ cup) salted water, cover and cook on HIGH for 6-8 minutes until just tender. Take care not to overcook cauliflower or it will become soft and loose its texture. Drain and turn out carefully into a heat resistant dish and coat with the sauce. Mix the breadcrumbs and ham together and sprinkle over the top. Brown under the grill.
Serves 3-4

Tolhouse Baked Beans

2-1 lb. 2 oz. cans baked beans
  (New England style)
1 lb. can (solid pack) tomatoes
4 oz. bacon, cooked and crumbled
2 oz. (½ cup) onion, chopped

1 ½ tablespoons (2T) black treacle
  (molasses)
½ oz. (1T) sugar
2 teaspoons dry mustard
cooked onion rings, to garnish

Pour the beans into a 2 quart heat resistant casserole.

Combine the tomatoes with the remaining ingredients, stir into the beans. Cover and cook on HIGH for 10 minutes, stirring after 5 minutes. Leave to stand for 10 minutes before serving. Garnish with onion rings.

Serves 6-8

Wilted Spinach Salad

1 lb. fresh spinach
6 slices bacon
2 tablespoons (3T) onion, finely
  chopped
¼ teaspoon pepper

1 ½ tablespoons (2T) sugar
4 tablespoons (⅓ cup) wine
  vinegar
2 tablespoons (3T) finely chopped
  pimento

Wash the spinach carefully and remove any thick stems and bruised leaves. Drain well and place in a salad bowl.

Put the bacon in a heat resistant dish, cover with a piece of absorbent kitchen paper and cook on HIGH for 5 minutes or until crisp. Remove the bacon, crumble and set aside. Add the onion to the bacon fat and cook uncovered on HIGH for 2 minutes until lightly browned.

To make the dressing, combine the remaining ingredients with 4 tablespoons (⅓ cup) water and heat uncovered on HIGH for 3 minutes or until the mixture comes to the boil.

Just before serving, pour the boiled dressing over the spinach.

Add the bacon and toss well.

Serve at once.

Serves 2

CAKES, DESSERTS AND BREAD

Watching a cake rise in the microwave oven is as spectacular as witnessing an Olympic high diver. You hold your breath and wonder if it will be successful and inevitably it is. Chocolate cakes, ginger cakes and fruit cakes require no embellishment, but because the microwave oven does not brown, some form of decoration is needed on plain cake mixtures. Icings and frostings, almond paste, nuts, jam, glacé cherries are just a few suggestions. If you are in a hurry either add a few drops of lemon colouring to the basic mixture or brown the cake lightly under the grill.

Cake dishes may either be greased and lined in the conventional way or lined with plastic film loosely fitted inside the container. Cakes are cooked when just dry on top.

Nearly all desserts can be prepared by microwave whether they be jellies, creams, charlottes or crumbles. Pastry should first be baked blind, weighting the centre with a saucer resting on a piece of absorbent kitchen paper. Continue cooking after filling if necessary.

Proving and rising bread doughs may be hastened by giving a few seconds in the microwave oven intermittently. To obtain a crusty finish, either pop the bread into a hot conventional oven for a few minutes or brown under the grill. Both bread and cakes should be baked in deep containers. If containers are too shallow, the mixture will rise and topple over the sides. Add a little extra liquid to bread and cake mixtures to obtain the best results in microwave cookery.

64   CRÈME BRÛLÉE (*page 66*)

Crème Brûlée

8 fl. oz. (1 cup) double (heavy)
  cream
8 fl. oz. (1 cup) milk
2 teaspoons granulated sugar
1 tablespoon (1½T) vanilla
  essence

3 egg yolks, beaten
4 tablespoons (⅓ cup) brown
  sugar
2 oz. shelled almonds, toasted

Combine the cream, milk, granulated sugar and vanilla essence. Strain in the egg yolks and stir well. Pour the mixture into a 1½ pint (3¾ cup) soufflé dish or other heat resistant dish. Stand in a shallow heat resistant casserole, half filled with boiling water.

Cook on LOW for 16-18 minutes, stirring twice during the first 5 minutes. The crème will be cooked when a knife inserted into the centre comes out clean. Remove the dish from the water.

Leave to cool, then chill for at least 4 hours.

Sprinkle the brown sugar over the chilled crème. Put under a hot grill until the sugar has dissolved and caramelized. Top with toasted almonds. Refrigerate for 3 hours before serving.

Serves 3

In a microwave oven without variable control of 650 watts output or over, the crème must be cooked in individual dishes. Divide the mixture between 3 individual soufflé dishes. Place in a heat resistant dish, half filled with boiling water. Cook for 4½-5 minutes until the mixture starts to bubble. The custards will set as they cool.

Baked Honey Apples

4 cooking (tart) apples
1½ oz. (3T) butter
2 oz. (¼ cup) soft (light) brown
 sugar

1 oz. (3T) raisins
2 tablespoons (3T) chopped nuts
3 tablespoons (¼ cup) water
1½ tablespoons (2T) thin honey

Wash and core the apples and score round the middle with a sharp knife. Put the butter, sugar, raisins and nuts in a bowl and mix well. Press quarter of the stuffing into each cavity and put the apples into individual heat resistant serving dishes.

Mix the water and honey together and spoon over the apples.

Cover each apple with waxed or greaseproof paper, put the dishes into the microwave oven and cook on HIGH for 6-8 minutes until tender.

Cooking times vary considerably depending on the size and ripeness of the fruit. Cooking continues after the oven is switched off, so do not be tempted to overcook.
Serves 4

Cherry and Walnut Cake

6 oz. (¾ cup) butter
3 oz. (6T) soft (light) brown sugar
2 oz. (3T) honey
6 eggs
3 oz. (¾ cup) flour
¾ teaspoon salt
¾ teaspoon baking powder
¾ teaspoon ground nutmeg

¾ teaspoon ground allspice
5 tablespoons (6T) brandy
1 lb. 8 oz. (6 cups) walnuts,
 coarsely chopped
1 lb. 12 oz. (3½ cups) mixed green
 and red glacé (candied) cherries,
 washed and dried

Cream the butter and sugar until light and fluffy.

Stir in the honey, then beat in the eggs, one at a time.

Sift in the flour, salt, baking powder, nutmeg and allspice and beat until smooth.

Mix in the brandy, walnuts and cherries. Turn the batter into a deep soufflé dish. Cover with a sheet of waxed or greaseproof paper and cook on MEDIUM for 16-18 minutes until a skewer comes out clean.

Leave to stand for 20 minutes before turning out onto a rack.

If desired, coat with glacé icing.
Makes one 6-7 inch cake
For best results all the ingredients should be at room temperature. This cake may be cooked on HIGH for 6-8 minutes, but will not taste as moist and fruity.

Fruit Surprise Pudding

3 oz. (⅓ cup) butter
8 oz. (1 cup) sugar
10 oz. (2½ cups) flour
2 teaspoons baking powder
½ teaspoon salt
8 fl. oz. (1 cup) milk
1 teaspoon vanilla essence
4 oz. (½ cup) maraschino cherries,
  drained and chopped

8 oz. can crushed pineapple,
  drained
½ oz. (1T) butter
8 oz. (1 cup) soft (light) brown
  sugar
¼ pint (⅔ cup) double (heavy)
  cream, whipped

Cream the butter and sugar until light and fluffy.
    Sift the flour, baking powder and salt together.
    Combine the milk and vanilla essence. Add the dry ingredients alternately with the milk to the creamed mixture. Spread the mixture in a buttered 2 quart heat resistant dish. Sprinkle with the cherries and pineapple and dot with butter. Cover the fruit with an even layer of brown sugar. Pour ¼ pint (⅔ cup) boiling water over. Cover with waxed paper or non-stick vegetable parchment. Cook on HIGH for 10-12 minutes, giving the dish a quarter turn every 2½ minutes. Leave to stand covered for 10 minutes before serving.
    Serve the pudding in individual dishes. Top each with a generous spoonful of whipped cream.
Serves 8

Gooseberry Oat Pie

1½ lb. (4 cups) gooseberries
8 oz. (1 cup) granulated sugar
5 oz. (1¼ cups) flour
½ teaspoon ground ginger

1¾ oz. (½ cup) porridge (rolled)
  oats
8 oz. (1 cup) brown sugar
4 oz. (½ cup) butter

Combine the gooseberries, granulated sugar, 1 oz. (¼ cup) of the flour, ginger and 6 tablespoons (½ cup) water in a deep heat resistant dish. Cover with plastic film and cook on HIGH for 4 minutes. Mix the remainder of the flour, oats and brown sugar together and rub in the butter.
    Spread this mixture over the gooseberries and cook uncovered on HIGH for 6-8 minutes until the topping is golden and crispy.
Serves 8

Cheesecake

8 oz. (2 cups) digestive biscuits
  (graham crackers), crushed
14 oz. (1¾ cups) sugar
4 oz. (½ cup) butter
½ teaspoon cinnamon

1½ lb. cream cheese
5 eggs, beaten
2 teaspoons vanilla essence
1 pint (2½ cups) soured cream

Combine the crushed biscuits, 4 oz. (½ cup) of the sugar, butter and cinnamon in a 13 × 9 × 2 inch dish. Press into the bottom of the dish. Cook on HIGH for 2 minutes. Beat the cream cheese until smooth. Mix in the eggs a little at a time, then add 8 oz. (1 cup) sugar and ½ teaspoon of the vanilla essence. Pour over the biscuit base. Cook on HIGH for 15 minutes, giving the dish a quarter turn every 4 minutes. Combine the soured cream with the remaining sugar and vanilla essence and blend well. Pour the mixture over the cheesecake, return to the oven and cook for 1 minute 15 seconds. Chill in the refrigerator.

Put this cake in the freezer for a few hours. It will then be easier to remove from its oblong pan for slicing.

Serves 10-12

Marzipan Orange Cup Cakes

3 oz. (6T) butter
3 oz. (6T) sugar
2 eggs, beaten
5 oz. (1¼ cups) flour
¼ teaspoon baking powder
pinch salt

1 teaspoon grated orange peel
1 tablespoon (1T) orange juice
apricot jam
8 oz. marzipan
icing (confectioners') sugar

Cream the butter and sugar together until light and fluffly.

Beat in the eggs a little at a time. Sift the flour, baking powder and salt, add the orange peel and fold this into the creamed mixture alternately with the orange juice. Using a teaspoon, half fill 12 paper cake cases.

Cook 6 at a time, well spread out, on HIGH for 2½-3 minutes.

Spread apricot jam on top of the cakes while they are still warm.

Roll out the marzipan to a thickness of ¼ inch on a board sprinkled with icing sugar. Cut out rounds to fit the diameter of the cakes and place on top of the jam.

Makes 12

Use two paper cases, one inside the other, to help the cakes keep their shape during cooking. Do not burn cup cakes, which cook very quickly due to the small amount of mixture in each.

Sticky Buns

14 oz. packet bread (hot roll) mix
3 oz. (⅓ cup) butter
4 oz. (½ cup) granulated sugar
½ teaspoon ground cinnamon

4 oz. (½ cup) soft (light) brown
  sugar
2 oz. (½ cup) walnuts, chopped

Prepare the mix according to the directions on the packet and leave to rise.

Divide the dough into 2 equal parts. Roll out each half to an 8 × 16 inch rectangle on a floured board. Cook the butter on HIGH for 1 or 2 minutes until melted. Brush each rectangle with a little melted butter and sprinkle with the sugar and cinnamon.

Roll up like a Swiss roll (jelly roll) from the long side and cut each roll into 8 pieces. Divide the remaining butter between two 9 inch cake pans and sprinkle with the brown sugar and walnuts. Arrange the buns cut side up around the sides of the pans, cover and leave to rise for 15 minutes.

Cook each pan uncovered on HIGH for 8 minutes until a skewer comes out clean. Give the pan ¼ turn every 2 minutes during cooking. Leave to cool for 5 minutes before turning onto a baking tray. Spoon any residual syrup over the buns which may then be browned under the grill.
Makes 16

Wholewheat Bread

1 oz. (1 cake) fresh yeast
¾ pint (2 cups) milk
1 tablespoon (1T) salt
1 oz. (2T) butter

3 oz. (¼ cup) black treacle
  (molasses)
1½ lb. (6 cups) wholewheat flour

Dissolve the yeast in 3 tablespoons (¼ cup) water. Add the milk, salt, butter, black treacle and wholewheat flour. Knead well, adding more flour if necessary to prevent the dough from sticking to the hands. Put the dough in a large buttered bowl covered tightly with plastic film.

Cook on MEDIUM for 30 seconds to speed rising. Remove from the oven and leave until the dough has doubled its size. Knock back and shape into 2 loaves. Press each loaf into an ungreased 8 × 4 inch glass loaf pan. Cover and leave to rise for 15 minutes. Cook separately on HIGH for 6-8 minutes, giving the pan ¼ turn every 1½-2 minutes. Brown on all sides under the grill.
Makes 2 loaves

CANDIES AND COOKIES

Home made confectionery is always exciting to make. Many recipes are based on syrups and if these boil over in the microwave oven, cleaning up is far easier than when a similar disaster occurs on the conventional hob. Nevertheless, many recipes call for exact temperatures and these must be tested with a sugar thermometer. This must never be left in the microwave oven by mistake, as it would either damage the magnetron or itself. Reliable tests can also be made by dropping a little of the mixture into cold water.

Recipes in this chapter include both the sugar candy type and mixtures that require little attention. Choose cookie and biscuits mixtures that have some coloured ingredients or decorate when cool. Bake biscuit mixtures in a box and cut into squares after cooking or form into separate balls or shapes and bake a few at a time on a sheet of non-stick vegetable parchment. Candies and biscuits often appear undercooked when in fact they are ready. Leave them to cool before testing and then give an extra boost in the microwave oven if necessary.

When a recipe calls for chocolate chips or bits, any chocolate can be substituted, but you may find that plain chocolate melts more evenly than milk chocolate. Some special chocolate dots are available which are extremely slow to melt, but these are most impressive when incorporated into plain cookie mixtures.

Light corn syrup is halfway between golden syrup and glucose syrup. Light corn syrup is difficult to obtain in the United Kingdom, yet the other syrups are hard to come by in America. If neither light corn syrup nor glucose syrup is obtainable golden syrup may be substituted.

FRUITED COOKIE SQUARES (*page 74*)

Fruited Cookie Squares

6 oz. (1 cup) mixed dried fruit or
  chopped dates or glacé cherries
4 oz. (1 cup) pecans or walnuts,
  chopped
6 oz. (1 cup) soft (light) brown
  sugar
3 oz. (¾ cup) flour

1½ teaspoons baking powder
¼ teaspoon salt
3 eggs
1 teaspoon vanilla essence
cinnamon
sugar

Thoroughly mix the fruit, nuts, sugar, flour, baking powder and salt together.

Beat the eggs with 1½ tablespoons (2T) water and vanilla essence, then stir into the fruit mixture, blending thoroughly. Turn into an 8 × 8 × 2 inch buttered dish and cover loosely with plastic film. Cook on HIGH for about 8 minutes, giving the dish a turn at two minute intervals. Leave to rest for 10 minutes, then turn out onto a rack. Cut into squares and sprinkle with cinnamon and sugar.

Makes 16

Peanut Brittle

1½ teaspoons bicarbonate of soda
  (baking soda)
1 teaspoon vanilla essence
12 oz. (1½ cups) sugar

5½ oz. (1 cup) glucose syrup (light
  corn syrup)
1½ oz. (3T) butter
1 lb. peanuts, shelled and skinned

Combine the bicarbonate of soda, 1 teaspoon water and vanilla essence in a small bowl. Stir the sugar, 8 fl. oz. (1 cup) water and syrup together in a deep 3 quart heat resistant bowl. Cook uncovered on HIGH for 15 minutes until a sugar thermometer registers 240°F, 115°C or a teaspoonful of the syrup forms a soft ball when dropped into cold water. Stir in the butter until melted.

Add the peanuts and cook uncovered on HIGH for 20 minutes until the sugar thermometer registers 300°F, 150°C, when a teaspoonful of mixture dropped into cold water separates into hard brittle threads. Stir occasionally with a wooden spoon.

While the peanut mixture is heating, grease two baking sheets and warm in a conventional oven at 250°F, Gas Mark ½.

Stir the reserved soda mixture into the hot peanut syrup and spread over the baking sheets to a depth of ¼ inch.

Break the peanut brittle into bite sized pieces when cool.

Makes about 1½ lb.

Fluffy Marshmallow

¼ oz. (1 envelope) unflavoured
  powdered gelatine
4 tablespoons (⅓ cup) cold water
4 oz. (½ cup) sugar

3½ oz. (1 cup) glucose syrup (light
  corn syrup)
½ teaspoon vanilla essence
icing (confectioners') sugar

Sprinkle the gelatine over the cold water in a large heat resistant bowl.
Cook on HIGH for about 45 seconds until the gelatine dissolves.

Stir in the sugar and heat briefly until dissolved, then add the syrup and
vanilla essence. Beat with an electric mixer for about 15 minutes or until
the mixture is very thick and resembles marshmallow.

Turn into an 8 inch square tin, generously coated with icing sugar. Leave
to stand at room temperature for about 1 hour until set.

Turn onto a board, sprinkled with plenty of icing sugar and cut into 1
inch squares with a knife dipped in cold water.

Toss marshmallows in icing sugar.
Makes 64

Penuche

1 lb. 2 oz. (3 cups) soft (light)
  brown sugar
½ pint (1 ¼ cups) milk
2 tablespoons (3T) butter

pinch salt
1 teaspoon vanilla essence
pinch cream of tartar
2 oz. (½ cup) nuts, chopped

Combine the sugar, milk, butter, salt and vanilla essence in a 3 quart heat
resistant bowl. Cook on HIGH, stirring occasionally, until the sugar is
dissolved, about 5 or 6 minutes.

Stir well, then continue cooking until a sugar thermometer registers
240°F, 115°C, when a teaspoonful of the mixture dropped in cold water
will form a soft ball.

Stir in the cream of tartar, then beat vigorously until the mixture is thick
and creamy. Stir in the nuts and pour the mixture into a buttered 9 inch
square tin. Cut into cubes when cold.
Makes 18

Merry Mints

1½ oz. (3T) butter
2 tablespoons (3T) milk
15½ oz. packet creamy white
  frosting mix

½ teaspoon peppermint extract
pink and green food colouring

Put the butter and milk in a 1½ quart heat resistant bowl.
    Heat on HIGH for 1 minute until the butter melts. Stir in the frosting mix. Cook uncovered on HIGH for 1½-2 minutes until the mixture bubbles. Stir frequently.
    Add the peppermint. Divide the mixture in two, colouring one half green and the other pink.
    Place teaspoonsfuls of the mixture on waxed paper or non-stick vegetable parchment and leave until set.
Makes 40
Substitute icing sugar (confectioners' sugar) and a pinch of cream of tartar if frosting mix is not obtainable.

Divinity

1½ lb. (3 cups) granulated sugar
2 oz. (½ cup) glucose syrup (light
  corn syrup)
¼ teaspoon salt

2 egg whites
¼ teaspoon vanilla essence
4 oz. (1 cup) nuts, chopped

Put the sugar, syrup and ¼ pint (⅔ cup) water in a 3 quart heat resistant bowl and cook uncovered on HIGH for 12-12½ minutes until a sugar thermometer reads 300°F, 150°C or a teaspoonful of mixture separates into hard brittle threads when dropped into cold water.
    Add the salt to the egg whites and whisk until stiff. Slowly pour the syrup in a thin stream into the egg whites, beating constantly until the mixture loses its shine and thickens.
    Stir in the vanilla and nuts. Drop teaspoonsfuls of the mixture at once on to waxed paper or non-stick vegetable parchment.
Makes 30

MERRY MINTS, DIVINITY, FANTASTIC FUDGE (page 78)

Fantastic Fudge

2 lb. (4 cups) granulated sugar
14 oz. can evaporated milk
8 oz. (1 cup) butter
12 oz. plain (semi-sweet)
  chocolate chips

7 oz. jar marshmallow cream
1 teaspoon vanilla essence
4 oz. (1 cup) walnuts, chopped
walnut halves for decoration

Combine the sugar, milk and butter in a 4 quart heat resistant bowl. Cook uncovered on HIGH for 18-20 minutes until a sugar thermometer registers 240°F, 115°C or a teaspoonful of the mixture dropped into cold water forms a soft ball. Stir frequently during cooking and watch carefully to avoid the mixture boiling over.

Mix in the chocolate and marshmallow cream. Stir until well blended. Add the vanilla and chopped nuts. Pour into a buttered 9 inch square dish. Cool and cut into squares. Decorate with walnut halves.

Makes 25-35

If marshmallow cream is not available, halve the quantity of sugar and add 16 marshmallows cut in half when cooking the sugar, milk and butter.

Almond Crescents

4 oz. (1 cup) shelled almonds,
  finely grated
5 oz. (1¼ cups) flour
1 oz. (¼ cup) icing (confectioners')
  sugar, sifted

4 oz. (½ cup) butter
1 egg yolk

Combine the almonds, flour and icing sugar.

Work in the butter and egg yolk, using one hand, until the mixture is well blended and forms a soft paste. Wrap in plastic film and chill until firm. Pinch off pieces of dough the size of walnuts and shape into crescents. Place 8 at a time well spread out on a sheet of waxed paper or non-stick vegetable parchment.

Cook on HIGH for about 2 minutes.

Makes 24

Chocolate Bourbon Balls

4 oz. (1 cup) pecans or walnuts,
  finely chopped
3 tablespoons (¼ cup) bourbon
  whisky
4 oz. (½ cup) butter

1 lb. 2 oz. (4 cups) icing
  (confectioners') sugar, sifted
1½ lb. plain (semi-sweet)
  chocolate chips

Combine the nuts with the bourbon. Cover and refrigerate overnight. Put the butter in a small heat resistant bowl and cook on HIGH for 1 minute until melted. Gradually stir in the sugar and then add the nuts and whisky, mixing well. Refrigerate until the mixture is firm enough to hold its shape for dipping. Add more sugar if the mixture is not stiff enough. Put the chocolate into a heat resistant bowl and cook on HIGH for about 4 minutes until melted.

While the chocolate is melting, shape the mixture into balls. Arrange the balls on a tray lined with waxed paper or non-stick vegetable parchment and return to the refrigerator to harden. Spear each ball with a wooden cocktail stick and dip into the melted chocolate. Replace on the paper and refrigerate.

Only dip a few bourbon balls at a time, leaving the remainder in the refrigerator. If the balls become too soft, put them back in the refrigerator to harden. Should the chocolate become too stiff, cook on HIGH for 1 minute to soften.
Makes 18

French Chocolates

12 oz. plain (semi-sweet)
  chocolate chips
4 oz. (1 cup) walnuts, ground
generous ¼ pint (¾ cup)
  sweetened condensed milk

1 teaspoon vanilla essence
pinch salt
chocolate strands
shredded coconut
chopped nuts

Put the chocolate into a medium sized heat resistant bowl and cook uncovered on HIGH for 4 minutes until melted.

Stir in the nuts, milk, vanilla essence and salt. Leave to cool for 5 minutes. Roll into balls and coat with chocolate strands, coconut or nuts as desired. Place on a greased baking sheet and refrigerate until set.
Makes 40-50

SAUCES AND PRESERVES

Direct heat is the enemy of a good sauce. When conventionally prepared in a saucepan, continuous stirring is required if lumps are to be avoided. Magical microwave has no direct heat, so that saucepans cannot burn on the bottom.

Roux based sauces are cooked in the well tried traditional sequence, but each step is carried out in the microwave oven. Bowls must be large to prevent boiling over and sauces should be stirred every half minute. A good basic sauce should be smooth and have a silky sheen. This is exactly the result you will have when sauces are cooked by microwave. If cornflour is used in place of flour, only half the weight in ratio to the liquid should be used. Stir the cornflour into part of the cold liquid before adding to the remaining mixture, then bring to the boil, stirring occasionally until the sauce thickens. Fruit sauces can also be thickened with arrowroot, applying the same method.

Emulsified sauces are normally prepared in a double saucepan on the conventional hob. There is no need for this in microwave cookery, but it is imperative not to overcook, because this type of sauce curdles easily. Make up the smallest quantities that you require and use a MEDIUM or LOW setting if you have an oven with variable control. Hollandaise and similar egg and butter based sauces should be cooked in the serving jug, making it easier to pour and preventing waste. Make sure that the jug is large enough.

Jams should also be cooked in the largest available bowl which must be resistant to high temperature cooking. Approximately 5 pounds can be made at any one time, although it is often convenient to make 'just enough for tea'. Fruit with a high pectin content should be softened before the sugar is added and a pre-soak period is helpful in producing a better gel. Fruit curds and cheeses are simple to make but do not keep very well, so unless you own a freezer, make only the quantity needed for fairly immediate use.

Unless jam is to be stored for a very long time, old fashioned waxed discs and jam pot covers are not necessary. A loose covering of plastic film placed on each filled pot then microwaved for a minute will, when cool form a perfect seal.

80   CHERRY SAUCE, *page 86 (Photograph: Panasonic)*

Hollandaise Sauce

4 oz. (½ cup) butter
3 egg yolks
1 tablespoon (1T) lemon juice

¼ teaspoon salt
¼ teaspoon dry mustard

Cut the butter into pieces and cook on LOW for 25 to 30 seconds until soft but not melted. Beat the egg yolks with the lemon juice, salt and mustard and strain into the softened butter. Stir well. Cover the bowl with waxed or greaseproof paper and cook on LOW for 15 seconds. Stir.

Cook for a further 20 seconds, stir and repeat until the sauce is hot. Remove from the oven and beat until light.

The sauce may be stored covered in the refrigerator and reheated in the microwave oven on HIGH for about 1½ minutes.

Makes ⅓ pint (¾ cup)

On microwave ovens without variable control and with an output of 650 watts or more, cook on HIGH for only 5 or 10 seconds during each cooking period.

White Sauce

1 oz. (2T) butter
1 oz. (¼ cup) flour

½ pint (1 cup) milk
salt, pepper

Put the butter in a large heat resistant bowl and cook on HIGH for about 30 seconds until the butter is melted. Blend in the flour, stirring until smooth, then cook for a further 30 seconds. Gradually stir in the milk, then cook for 2½-3 minutes until the sauce thickens. Stir occasionally.

Add salt and pepper to taste.

Makes ½ pint (1 cup)

Increase the quantity and lengthen the cooking time slightly if a thinner sauce is required.

This sauce can be used as a basis for endless variations. Try the following suggestions:—

Cheese sauce — add 1-2 oz. grated cheese.

Egg sauce — add 2 chopped hard boiled eggs and 1 teaspoon lemon juice.

Onion sauce — add 1 tablespoon chopped onion.

Mushroom sauce — add 2-3 tablespoons cooked, chopped mushrooms.

Barbecue Sauce

1½ tablespoons (2T) butter
1 medium onion, finely chopped
1 clove garlic, crushed
2 tablespoons (3T) finely chopped
  green pepper
generous ¼ pint (¾ cup) tomato
  ketchup (catsup)
3 tablespoons (¼ cup) water

3 tablespoons (¼ cup) cider
  vinegar
¼ teaspoon dry mustard
2 oz. (¼ cup) soft (light) brown
  sugar
¼ teaspoon salt
few drops Tabasco sauce

Put the butter, onion, garlic and green pepper into a large heat resistant bowl. Cook on HIGH for about 3 minutes until the onion is tender. Stir occasionally. Mix in the remaining ingredients. Continue cooking uncovered for about 2 minutes until the sauce bubbles.

Serve this sauce with meat or poultry.

Makes 1 pint (2½ cups)

Oriental Sauce

4 tablespoons (⅓ cup) soy sauce
2 tablespoons (3T) cornflour
  (cornstarch)
10 oz. can concentrated
  consommé

½ pint (1¼ cups) water
2 tablespoons (3T) dry sherry
¼ teaspoon ground ginger
1 clove garlic, crushed

Put the soy sauce in a large heat resistant bowl and blend in the cornflour. Gradually stir in the consommé, water, sherry, ginger and garlic, mixing well so that the cornflour does not remain on the bottom of the bowl. Cook on HIGH for 4-5 minutes until the sauce is clear. Stir occasionally.

Serve with cubes of cooked pork or chicken.

Makes 1 pint (2½ cups)

Creole Sauce

2 oz. (½ cup) onion, chopped
1 oz. (¼ cup) green pepper,
  chopped
1 oz. (¼ cup) celery, chopped
1 oz. (2T) butter

1 tomato, peeled and chopped
8 oz. can tomato sauce
3 oz. can mushrooms, undrained
¼ teaspoon salt
pinch of garlic powder

Combine the onion, pepper, celery and butter in a large heat resistant bowl. Cook uncovered for 4 minutes until the vegetables are tender. Stir in the remaining ingredients. Cover and cook for a further 5 minutes.

Serve on cooked fish or vegetables.

Makes 1 pint (2½ cups)

If canned tomato sauce is unobtainable substitute 4 tablespoons (⅓ cup) tomato purée blended with ¼ pint (⅔ cup) water.

Sweet 'n' Sour Sauce

14 oz. can pineapple chunks,
  undrained
generous ¼ pint (¾ cup) chicken
  stock or bouillon
1½ tablespoons (2T) brown sugar
3 tablespoons (¼ cup) vinegar
2 teaspoons soy sauce
1 teaspoon tomato ketchup
  (catsup)

1½ tablespoons (2T) cornflour
  (cornstarch)
2 oz. (½ cup) spring onions
  (scallions), sliced
1 green pepper, cut into 1 inch
  pieces

Drain the pineapple syrup into a large heat resistant bowl. Set the pineapple chunks aside. Add the stock, sugar, vinegar, soy sauce, ketchup and cornflour and stir well. Cook on HIGH for about 4 minutes until thickened. Stir frequently. Add the pineapple, onion and green pepper and cook for a further 30 seconds.

Serve with shrimps, pork or chicken.

Makes 1¼ pints (3 cups)

CREOLE SAUCE, SWEET 'N' SOUR SAUCE, LEMON FILLING
(page 86)

Lemon Filling

6 oz. (¾ cup) sugar
1½ tablespoons (2T) cornflour
  (cornstarch)
generous ¼ pint (¾ cup) water

3 tablespoons (¼ cup) lemon juice
½ teaspoon grated lemon peel
2 egg yolks, lightly beaten
1 oz. (2T) butter

Blend the sugar, cornflour and water together in a large heat resistant bowl. Stir in the lemon juice and peel, and cook on HIGH for about 3 minutes until the mixture clears. Stir every 30 seconds. Mix 2 or 3 spoonfuls of the mixture with the eggs, then return it to the mixing bowl. Stir and continue cooking for 1 minute, stirring again after 30 seconds.

Add the butter and leave to cool for several minutes before using as a cake or pie filling.

Filling for one 8 or 9 inch cake

Cherry Sauce

17 oz. can stoned black cherries
1 tablespoon (1T) cornflour
  (cornstarch)

1½ teaspoons lemon juice
1 teaspoon grated lemon peel

Drain the cherry juice into a large heat resistant bowl. Set the cherries aside. Blend the cornflour into the juice until smooth.

Cook uncovered on HIGH for about 4 minutes until thickened and clear. Stir occasionally to prevent lumps forming. Add the cherries, lemon juice and peel and stir well. Continue cooking for about 1 minute until the sauce bubbles and the cherries are hot.

Spoon over ice cream or cake.

Makes ¾ pint (2 cups)

Butterscotch Fondue Sauce

6 tablespoons (½ cup) evaporated
  milk
9 oz. (1½ cups) soft (light) brown
  sugar

1½ oz. (3T) butter
1½ tablespoons (2T) rum or
  brandy

Combine the milk, sugar and butter in a large heat resistant jug. Cook on HIGH for 4-5 minutes until the sugar is completely dissolved. Stir occasionally. Stir in the rum and cool slightly. Pour into a fondue pot and serve at the table, warming the pot over a low flame and use as a dip for cookies and cakes.

This sauce can also be poured over ice cream or puddings. It will store well in the refrigerator in a jar in which it can then be reheated.

Makes ½ pint (1¼ cups)

Chocolate Sauce

¼ pint (⅔ cup) water
2 oz. (¼ cup) sugar
½ teaspoon instant coffee powder
¼ teaspoon vanilla essence
2 oz. plain (semi-sweet) chocolate
  chips
1 teaspoon cornflour (cornstarch)
1 tablespoon milk

Put the water into a medium sized heat resistant bowl. Cook on HIGH for 2 minutes. Add the sugar and stir until dissolved. Stir in the coffee and vanilla essence and cook for about 2 minutes until the mixture boils. Leave to cool slightly, then add the chocolate, stirring until it has melted. Blend the cornflour with the milk, add to the chocolate mixture and cook for 1-2 minutes until the sauce thickens. Stir occasionally.

This sauce should be of pouring consistency.

Makes ½ pint (1¼ cups)

Fresno Fruit Sauce

3 oz. (½ cup) raisins
6 tablespoons (½ cup) water
3 tablespoons (¼ cup) redcurrant
  jelly
6 tablespoons (½ cup) orange
  juice
2 oz. (¼ cup) brown (firmly
  packed) sugar
1 tablespoon cornflour
  (cornstarch)
pinch of allspice

Combine the raisins, water, jelly and orange juice in a large heat resistant bowl. Heat for 3 minutes until the jelly melts, stirring once. Mix the sugar, cornflour and allspice together and stir into the raisin mixture. Cook for 1½ minutes, stirring every 30 seconds. Serve with baked ham, pork chops or duck.

Makes about ½ pint (1¼ cups)

Peach Conserve

2 breakfast cups (2 cups) chopped
  peaches
1 lb. 4 oz. can crushed pineapple,
  drained

8 oz. jar maraschino cherries,
  undrained
3¾ lb. (7½ cups) sugar
6 fl. oz. liquid fruit pectin (certo)

Combine the peaches, pineapple, chopped cherries and juice in a 4 quart heat resistant bowl. Cook uncovered on HIGH for 10 minutes.

Stir in the sugar and continue cooking uncovered for about 15 minutes until the mixture is boiling. Stir every 5 minutes.

Mix in the pectin and continue cooking for a further 10-15 minutes until a candy thermometer registers 220°F, 105°C. Stir for 5 minutes to cool, then pour into jars and seal.
Makes 3½ lb.

Strawberry Preserve

1 lb. packet of frozen strawberries
3 fl. oz. liquid pectin (certo)
  or 3 tablespoons powdered fruit
  pectin

1 lb. (2 cups) sugar
1 tablespoon lemon juice

Put the strawberries into a 2 quart heat resistant bowl. Cook on HIGH for 2 minutes. (If using powdered pectin, stir in at this stage). Cook for 2 minutes or until a few bubbles surface. Stir in sugar and lemon juice. Continue cooking for 6 minutes, stirring every 2 minutes. Stir in the liquid pectin. Allow to cool slightly for the fruit to settle. Pour into jars, seal and refrigerate.
Makes 1¼ pints (3 cups)

Grape Jelly

2 lb. (6 cups) fully ripe (concord)
 grapes
8 oz. (2 cups) cooking apples,
 diced

8 fl. oz. (1 cup) water
6 oz. (¾ cup) sugar for each ½ pint
 (cup) juice

Combine the grapes, apples and water in a 4 quart heat resistant bowl.
Cook covered on HIGH for 15-20 minutes until the fruit is tender. Stir
every 5 minutes. Strain the juice using several thicknesses of cheese cloth
or muslin. Measure the juice and return to the microwave oven. Bring to
the boil, about 10 minutes, then stir in the sugar. Cook for about 30
minutes until a sugar thermometer registers 220°F, 105°C or a drop of
syrup hangs to the side of a wooden spoon when tilted. Stir every 5
minutes. Pour into glasses to set. Seal.
Makes 1-1½ pints

Lemon Curd

3 oz. (6T) butter
6 oz. (¾ cup) sugar
2 teaspoons grated lemon rind

3 tablespoons (¼ cup) lemon juice
3 eggs, beaten

Put the butter in a large heat resistant bowl and cook on HIGH for 10 to 20
seconds until soft but not melted. Stir in the sugar, lemon rind and juice.
Strain the eggs into the bowl and blend well. Cover with waxed or
greaseproof paper and cook for 2½-3 minutes until thick. Stir every 30
seconds. Pour into a jar and leave to cool when the curd becomes thicker.
Store in a cool place.
Makes 1 lb. (1½ cups)

INDEX

INDEX

The editor would like to thank the following for their assistance in
compiling this book:-

*Litton Systems Inc., Panasonic, Tappan International
Photographs on pages 9, 21, 25, 29, 41, 69, 89 by courtesy of Amana Inc.
Photographs on pages 17, 45, 61, 73 by courtesy of Sharp Electronics Corporation
Photographs on frontispiece and pages 37, 77, 85 by courtesy of Thermidor*

PDO 82-1317